on equal terms

on equal terms

How to Make the Most of Learning Contracts in Grades 4-9

Scott C. Greenwood

NMSA
National Middle School Association

HEINEMANN
Portsmouth, NH

Heinemann
A division of Reed Elsevier Inc.
361 Hanover Street
Portsmouth, NH 03801–3912
www.heinemann.com

Offices and agents throughout the world

The author and publisher wish to thank those who have generously given permission to reprint borrowed material:

Figure 1–1 is reprinted from "Independent Study: A Flexible Tool for Academic and Personal Growth" by C.A. Tomlinson in *Middle School Journal*, 25 (1), 55–59. Copyright © 1993. Reprinted by permission of the National Middle School Association.

Figure 8–3 by Beth Jana Bondi is reprinted from *The New American Middle School: Educating Preadolescents in an Era of Change, 3rd Edition* by John Wiles and Joseph Bondi. Copyright © 2001 by Prentice-Hall, Inc. Reprinted by permission of Joseph Bondi.

Library of Congress Cataloging-in-Publication Data
Greenwood, Scott C.
  On equal terms : how to make the most of learning contracts in grades 4–9 /
Scott C. Greenwood.
      p. cm.
  Includes bibliographical references
  ISBN 0-325-00493-5 (pbk. : alk. paper)
  1. Learning contracts. 2. Elementary school teaching. 3. Middle school teaching.
I. Title.
LB1029.L43 G74 2003
371.139—dc21
                                                                                  2002151786

Editor: Lois Bridges
Production coordinator: Lynne Reed
Production service: Denise Botelho, Colophon
Cover design: Jenny Jensen Greenleaf
Cover photograph: Art Salatto
Interior photographs: Art Salatto
Typesetter: Argosy Publishing
Manufacturing: Steve Bernier

Printed in the United States of America on acid-free paper
07 06 05 04 03 VP 1 2 3 4 5

To the Nitschmann and E. T. Richardson kids
who taught me

Contents

Acknowledgments

This has been a labor of love; the process of making the invisible visible has been challenging and enlightening. I continue to have faith in kids, and in teachers who empower their children, still, in these high-stakes times.

I have had excellent writing models, in Perry Zirkel and George White at Lehigh University.

I have had the love and support of Leah, Alex, and Nathaniel. It has been a challenge and an adventure at times with the two boys, at ages three and five, who tacitly remind me that I'll never recapture these years of their lives.

I have had support and positive peer pressure from my colleagues at West Chester University's Literacy Department.

Melissa Bilbow, West Chester Graduate Assistant, has provided deeply appreciated word processing support, cogent feedback, and encouragement.

Contracting teachers Bev Tilhansky, Denise Mroz, Madeline O'Dowd, and Alicia Kalbach shared their products and processes. Chuck Menas, Donna Cattell, and Sue Shafer opened their doors to Art Salatto and me for photo opportunities.

Dave Brown of West Chester put me in touch with Lois Bridges. I've always been a consumer of Heinemann books, but recently I've gone back and paid attention to who edits the words of the stars. It's often Lois; she took on an unknown in me, and still provided honest feedback and individual attention and palpable encouragement. The woman rarely sleeps, by the way. My 7:00 AM emails were unexpectedly responded to immediately (4:00 in the morning in California!). With her work ethic as a model, how could I ever miss any deadlines? Whatever is good in this book is due to Lois' expertise and professionalism.

Introduction:
Why Contracting?

When a teacher tries to teach something to the entire class at the same time,
"chances are, one-third of the kids already know it; one-third will get it;
and the remaining third won't. So two-thirds of the children
are wasting their time."

—LILIAN KATZ
In Carol Tomlinson 1996
"Differentiating Instruction for
Mixed Ability Classrooms"
[An ASCD professional inquiry kit].
Alexandria VA: ASCD

Inservice does not conjure up wonderful connotations for most teachers. The conventional wisdom is that they'd hope to die during an inservice, so that the transition from life to death would be so subtle as to be barely discernible. But I got lucky as a newly minted prospective teacher… the district that had just employed me brought in a speaker/expert from (honestly) Slippery Rock College to tell us all about the power and possibilities of *learning contracts*. His name has long since left me, but he convinced me to give contracting a try, and a tweak, and more tries . . .

I have some stories and practicalities to share. Some years ago that unnamed Slippery Rock professor talked about the power of student choice and autonomy, with teacher guidance and control. I knew nothing of Nancie Atwell or James Beane, of the political frays, past, present, and future, pitting proponents of transmission against advocates of transaction. In retrospect, the Slippery Rock presenter was fairly behavioristic, as he compared the teacher–student contract to a mortgage or an automobile loan document, with clear and concise limits, payoffs, time frames, and sanctions.

What has endured for me is my belief that literacy learning is

- Social
- Recursive
- Personal
- Idiosyncratic

I believe that good teaching is a magical combination of art and science, that direct instruction is important but has to be targeted. And I firmly believe that children can be trusted to make good choices with a certain modicum of structure.

Vignette: November, of my first year of teaching; my ninth grade English class; western Pennsylvania (small district, first job). Dr. Moore, the superintendent, walks into my class unannounced to "observe"—unbeknownst to him, I had entered into a contract with four students to teach the novel *Death Be Not Proud*. They led the discussions, assigned the chapters, chose important vocabulary, wrote the final test, and were responsible for assessment. He walked in to see Nancy H. in the front of the class going over the final assessment, flanked by her three compatriots. I was sitting in a student desk, arguing vociferously about points that had been docked in an ambiguously (I thought so; the test makers did not) worded short essay—the committee of four was pleased to note that I did not get the highest grade in the class. Dr. Moore, after some explanation from me later, thought the observation was "interesting" but was concerned about peer evaluation, and he asked to come back another time to see a more traditional lesson that better matched the district-adopted observation checklist. Dr. Moore's contract was not renewed the following year.

No, at that time I was just beginning my graduate work, and I had not heard of Lilian Katz or Maxine Greene or Louise Rosenblatt. I had heard a little about

John Dewey and the progressive folks, but I mostly relied on instinct and my own memories of good instruction in my early years of teaching. I did not know the buzz words back then, but I had good intentions and a desire to enfranchise kids. Goodness knows I made some mistakes with that first batch of ninth graders, but we survived—together. As the years passed, I learned from students and they learned, likewise, from me. In the present political climate, it is important that educators remain client centered and reflective.

Students are most likely to be engaged in learning when they are active and are given some choice and control over the learning process—when the curriculum is authentic and relates to students' interests. Yet surveys of classroom practices reveal that instruction emphasizing rote learning and student passivity is the rule rather than the exception (Yair 2000). Contracting, as you shall see, provides the necessary structure to differentiate and customize. In the chapters that follow, you will learn about layering in literature circles, individualization, workshops, targeted mini lessons, and necessary whole class instruction. It can be done!

on equal terms

1

Contracting and Constructivism

What a bad teacher means by a good pupil is one who is docile, quiet, passive, and unquestioning; what a good teacher means by a bad pupil is one who is docile, quiet, passive and unquestioning...

—SYDNEY HARRIS

Learning contracts give the necessary balance and structure so that teachers have just enough control—but kids have control as well. This chapter provides the requisite theory and underpinnings to understand contracting.

History and Rationale

To me, teaching with contracts is a balance issue. Many of my own past teachers had practiced the *stevedore model* of teaching—pure transmission. They'd metaphorically back the empty trucks up to the loading docks and fill them up. The teachers were working hard, but the kids were not necessarily learning. Contracts foster student engagement; engaged students make a psychological investment in learning. They may, of course, take pride in earning formal indicators of success (grades), but they are also intrinsically motivated to learn. Engaged students are more likely to approach tasks eagerly and to persist in the face of difficulty. Conversely, learners who do not believe that they have control or choice are less likely to expend the effort necessary to learn.

The central rationale for contracting is this: What is the proper distribution of initiative and responsibility between teacher and student? A learning contract is simply a written agreement between teacher and learner in which the learner undertakes to complete mutually agreed upon tasks in a specified amount of time on his or her own initiative.

There are stylistic and philosophical reasons why teachers do not try contracts to differentiate instruction and help manage a workshop type of environment. Yet several common themes clearly support contracting:

- Teachers must have time and opportunity to work with individuals and small groups while other children are constructively occupied. When teachers are challenged to individualize and differentiate, the most frequent "Yeah, but" I've heard is "What am I supposed to have the other (fill in the number) do"?
- The uniqueness of children means that they learn in different ways, at different speeds, with varying levels of interest.
- Independence and initiative, balanced with abilities to synergize and work cooperatively, are traits to be fostered within the school environment—these are necessary for the world beyond schooling.
- Children are often required to waste large amounts of time waiting (for lessons, for materials, for instruction, for problems to be solved) rather than being enabled to get on with it. A colleague who became a contracting convert once joked about a "good girl" who kept a novel on her lap during his sixth grade class and was able to finish one a week during the aforementioned waiting times.

The early publication *Education on the Dalton Plan* (Parkhurst 1922) explains a laboratory system that began in the United States and then spread to schools in England. Parkhurst's book chronicled her experiences in attempting to organize a one-room country school, as well as her work with Maria Montessori in Italy, which culminated in her philosophy's application in the Dalton High School in Massachusetts. Her exhortation that "freedom is not license, still less indiscipline [It is]. . . in fact, the very reverse of both" (15) still speaks volumes.

Traditional learning and teaching are based on the "taxonomy of learning" developed by Benjamin Bloom. Educators who look to behavioral psychology to explain learning find a *science* that employs counting and measurement and variables under control. Research in the behavioral sense is based on the study of animals (or facsimile) in controlled laboratory settings. The empirical rigor of the recent National Institute of Child Health and Human Development research has exacerbated the reading wars. But we are not talking about pine tree seedlings that are meted out various quantities and combinations of light, temperature, water, and fertilizer. We're talking about complex, feeling, living, young people. Dudley-Marling and Murphy (2001) note the disquieting trend of squelching child-centered values and voices, as artistic literacy teaching takes a back seat to packaged curricula and standardized of instruction.

To oversimplify, behaviorist theory holds that children learn to read by first making sense of the smallest components of language (letters) and then progressing to larger units or chunks (blends, words, sentences). This orientation held sway in the fifties and sixties and still controls the interactions in many classrooms and is the foundation upon which most commercial curricula and basal reading programs are based. It is also easier for teachers to control kids who are expected to memorize information and regurgitate ideas and facts transmitted to them via lectures and textbooks. An educated person, according to the behavioral paradigm, is said to be one who has learned the necessary facts, one who is culturally literate.

Fast forward to the late 1970s, when most of the discussion on contracts appeared in the special education literature, as a way of coping with children with obviously specialized needs. In the 1980s the literature began to use gentler language such as *negotiation* and *empowering* the learner (Atwell 1987; Boomer 1983; Rief 1992). These authors, and many more, advocated that the learner meet the teacher at the point of that learner's interest, needs, and abilities, rather than in terms of a group's need or a preconceived curriculum timeline.

James Beane (1990) has been particularly influential and persuasive in advocating for transactive teaching. He believes it is misguided to see child-centered teaching and learning as the antithesis of teaching content and skills. The difference is that knowledge and skills are repositioned around student's interests or transposed to answer kids' questions. Content and skills are simply present in a more meaningful way, so that the scope and sequence charts come alive. According to Beane, teachers cannot rely on the formal curriculum guides to organize learning, because the interests of children have not been heard.

Additional support for differentiation has come from the work of Carol Tomlinson (1993) and Cathy Vatterott (1995), who advocate careful teacher diagnosis of readiness as tools to move students toward independence (Figure 1–1). Both of these authors mention my work on contracting (Greenwood 1985, 1995; White and Greenwood 1992) but do not go into the particulars of contract delivery. Teachers are expected, it seems, to "meet the range" but are not provided with the specific tools and strategies to do so. Tomlinson and Vatterott mention contracting as viable and useful, but practicalities are not provided. Differentiation of instruction is more than a hot term. If we are going to move forward pedagogically, structures such as learning contracts really need to become more common.

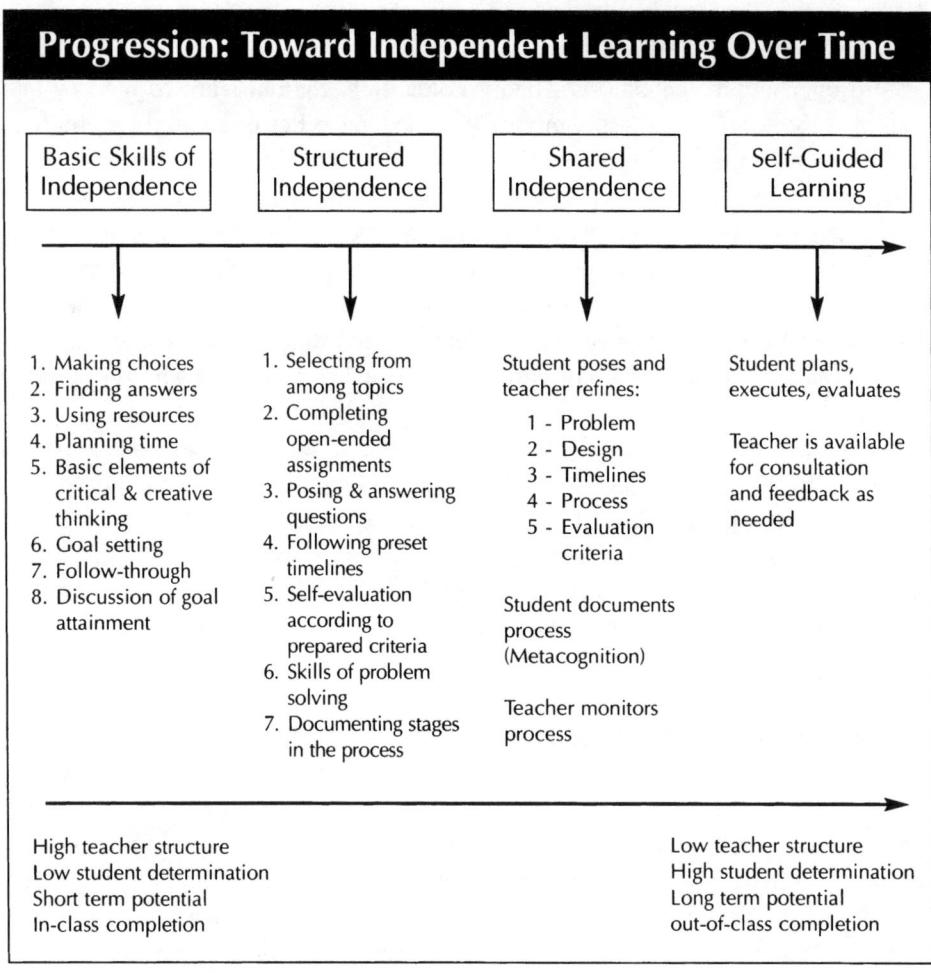

Figure 1–1. Carol Tomlinson's progression toward independent learning, used with permission from National Middle School Association. Tomlinson, C.A. 1993. Independent Study: A Flexible Tool for Academic and Personal Growth. *Middle School Journal*, 25: 55–59.

We are living in tricky political times. Those farthest removed from the exigencies and realities of the classroom are making decisions that are having profound effects on teachers and children. Promoting educational standards can be a very economical approach to school reform. Standards-based reform can be virtually cost-free, except for paying some hefty consultants' fees and providing room and board for some experts to retreat for a week or so. Susan Ohanian (1999) cautions about teachers getting locked into a view of themselves as technical experts.

Tales of teacher proofing and standardizing and homogenizing of curricula are frightening to those who recognize the quirks and predilections and individual needs of real children. For some educators unfortunately, "security is three checks on the board, seven steps in the lesson, and 178 state-issued competencies to get out of kindergarten" (Ohanian 1999, 11).

The authors of the powerful and timely *Best Practice* put it this way: "Achieving higher standards, by any realistic appraisal, requires paying for teacher training, materials, equipment—and probably outside-of school costs too, like improved child care and nutrition. But these solutions are so big, so broad, so costly that many people find it more comfortable to talk about 'raising the bar.' It costs far less to raise the bar than to help someone jump over it" (Zemelman, Daniels, and Hyde 1998, xi). Learning contracts provide children with the structure, security, and freedom to pursue their questions and dreams. Learners work to the application level and interact in more than a "just the facts, ma'am" mode. Trends in literacy learning come and go, but the power of student choice and motivation remains a constant.

A Special Fit in the Middle Grades

For this book, I take some liberty with the span of grades usually assumed to be middle level. Middle schools are typically comprised of sixth, seventh, and eighth graders, although many are 5, 6, 7, and 8 in span. I'd like to expand this book to include grades 4 though 9, although a corollary is that contracting has worked for me with graduate students, and I've seen contract learning being done well in first grade. However, let's broadly define *middle level* as spanning grades four through nine.

Those of us who know and love middle level students sometimes refer to them affectionately using semipejorative sobriquets: puberts, tweenagers, hormonally challenged individuals. Middle level guru Conrad Toepfer put it more gently when he told me, metaphorically, that "Crustaceans are most vulnerable when they are shedding their shells." Middle level teachers are well aware of the challenges and joys involved in working with, reaching, and sparking the needs of this magical and mystical age group.

As the middle level *movement* gained momentum during the 1980s and early 1990s there was an explosion of information regarding the unique nature of the middle level client in an effort to make middle level schools developmentally responsive and responsible, as opposed to the structure of the traditional *junior* high school model.

As researchers examined the physical, intellectual, social, and emotional needs of those in "the range of the strange," they were able to clearly delineate the rationale for middle school accoutrements such as block scheduling, exploratory programs, advisory programs, teaching teams, and the like.

The landmark *Turning Points* (Carnegie Council on Adolescent Development 1989) perhaps put it best when the authors said that developmentally sound and sensitive middle level schools are a potentially powerful force to recapture "millions of youth adrift" while also admitting that there exists a "volatile mismatch" between the organization and curriculum of many middle level schools and the special needs of most early adolescents.

It is my contention that even when some or most of the necessary structural components of true middle level schools are in place, instructionally (and most importantly, for this is where the rubber meets the road) many middle schools are often still junior highs in drag, where teacher-centered practices abound. Many pressures, rightfully perceived or otherwise, are felt by middle level teachers (Tracy and Greenwood 1991) from upper grade teachers, administrators, and parents to produce students who acquire the customary information in the customary manner. Despite the wonderful overt and covert successes of middle level teachers who have successfully negotiated the transition from being "sage on the stage" to "guide on the side," perhaps it is the persistence of teachers' underlying belief systems (Sparks and Hirsh 1997) about how students learn best that accounts for middle level instruction that still is not consonant with the needs of early adolescents.

A critical element in the successful implementation of differentiated instruction is, of course, the commitment and training of staff. At Silver Spring International Middle School in Maryland, for example, there has been a school-wide commitment to differentiated instruction—it follows that differentiation was the initial and primary focus of staff development. "The staff development effort has also been differentiated according to teacher needs and is based on their learning preferences" (Brimfield, Masci, and DeFiore 2002, 17).

With the knowledge base exploding and growing awareness (Hodgkinson 1992) that we cannot afford to waste any more young people, there is a clear and compelling need to recapture our middle level students' interests in learning, particularly in the vital communication arts. It is my contention that learning contracts are a conduit to meet the needs of both students and teachers alike, as the former spread their wings as learners and as the latter take risks in making the transition from the role of fillers of empty vessels to that of coaches and facilitators (Figures 1–2 and 1–3). As you will see shortly, the questions that kids ask, as outlined in Figure 1–2 are congruent with the developmental needs of middle level learners and can be addressed nicely via the framework of learning contracts. An accepting, supportive community of learners must be developed in order to meet those needs.

QUESTIONS STUDENTS ASK IN SCHOOL

- Do I feel accepted?
- Am I comfortable?
- Am I safe? How will the community respond to my mistakes, if I make them?
- Is this information useful to me?
- Can I do this?
- Do I know what is expected?
- Is this worth the risk?

MIDDLE LEVEL STUDENTS NEED

- Socialization
- Focus
- Movement
- Parameters/guidelines/structure
- Variety/choice
- Independence
- Talk

Figure 1–2. Questions students ask in school

The bottom of Figure 1–2 enumerates students' needs, specific to the stage of early adolescence. Those of us who know tweenagers well are accustomed to the inconsistencies of their needs. They crave structure and security and independence all at once or singly—when it suits them. Contracts help to balance these multiple needs. Figure 1–3 helps to further delineate the needs of these children. Please refer back to it as you delve into upcoming chapters. I have heard it said that if we don't find positive ways to meet the first two needs (recognition and acceptance; being taken seriously) they'll find their own ways to fit in and excel, often negative ways. Many teachers of literacy have embraced workshop tenets of instruction, but have gotten stuck on management and implementation issues. When risk-taking teachers meet opposition and resistance, they can be quick to revert back to old habits.

Additionally, contracting and differentiation must lose their special education mantle. Teachers must come to believe that strategies that help children with special needs help all children. "Good teachers [do] not have one best teaching method, but an arsenal of approaches appropriate in different circumstances"

(Kilgore, Griffin, Sindelar, and Webb 2002, 8). If inclusionary pressures are the *Trojan horse* that enables infusion of differentiation, the bottom line will be better student motivation and achievement. Kilgore and her colleagues cite a middle level principal who stated that "Inclusion…is not about students with disabilities—it's about whether educators are willing to accept responsibility for educating all students in a personalized and motivational way" (2002, 11). Similarly, differentiation (including contracting) is the school-wide goal of Silver Spring International Middle School, where Carol Tomlinson's model helps ensure that not only those identified as gifted and talented have access to challenging content and instruction (Brimfield, Masci, and DeFiore 2002). Flexible grouping is driven by ongoing assessment at Silver Spring, as student self-selection is woven throughout the fabric of the school.

Pitton (2001) notes the difficulties of truly reinventing middle level schools and schooling, even when adults are aware that a higher quality work product results when individuals have a say in what is completed and how it is accomplished. "Why is it so easy to tell young people to do rather than ask them?" (Pitton 2001, 15). She posits that asking for change that is child-centered is too

1. Recognition, acceptance as individual
2. Be taken seriously
3. Structure/security/safety
4. Freedom and flexibility to try new things
5. Information and help processing it (e.g., refusal skills)
6. Peer approval and acceptance
7. Ways to communicate to others (e.g., journals)
8. Outlets to release high energy

Figure 1–3. Specific needs of middle level child

much for many teachers to handle, that it moves them too far out of their comfort zones. She notes that the mismatch between the child's need for self-management and the opportunities provided for them in the classroom results in the students' lack of motivation and interest in school. "While many educators can recite a litany of young adolescent needs, their own reactions to the adolescents' push for independence and self-determination is often to squash the emerging sense of self with control and directives" (16).

Nancie Atwell (1999) reflected on her earlier teaching rather critically: "I didn't know how to share responsibility with my students and I wasn't too sure I wanted to. I liked the vantage of my big desk. . . . Wasn't that my job? If responsibility . . . shifted to my students, what would I do?" (13).

Most teachers understand that the middle grades' philosophy dovetails beautifully with a philosophy that advocates literacy learning that is child-centered, whole, and meaningful. They want to provide opportunities for meaningful reading, writing, listening, and speaking; however, they sometimes don't know how to get there. Student-centered practices (including contracting) in the middle grades are about empowerment of teachers as well as students. "Teachers who are disempowered themselves as professionals cannot empower students as learners" (Hoffman 1992, 368). Hoffman stated further that criterion-referenced testing, detailed lesson plans turned into the office in advance, fragmented curricula, and the like were still, unfortunately, used for accountability purposes. That was over ten years ago. We are now in the times of hyperaccountability, with test scores being used to mete out various sanctions and awards, from student promotion to teacher bonuses.

The use of learning contracts at the middle level requires reciprocal interaction in the classroom, encouragement of student interdependence, and a downplay of the teacher's traditional transmission role. Learning contracts empower students and allow them to assume greater control over their own learning by allowing them choice and freedom while at the same time providing structure and security. Concurrently, teachers gain more power by gradually relinquishing it. The learning contract is the ideal way for the teacher to raise levels of expectation, provide individual attention, and personalize the educational experience for young adolescents and facilitate genuine change in pupil–teacher interactions. Contracts really work. As the chapters unfold, join me in learning about a framework that empowers children and still provides a reasonable amount of teacher management and accountability.

2

Setting the Table: Management and Basics

To learn a particular concept, some children need days; some, ten minutes,
but the typical lockstep school schedule ignores this fundamental fact.
—MARILYN HUGHES

Linda Rief (1992) and Nancie Atwell (1999) both write of similar encounters with their own principals. After several years as a high school English teacher, I came to my first middle school mid-year and immersed myself in the lives of twelve year olds. My new principal was a very traditional, autocratic instructional leader. He was generally supportive when he was informed of and approved of practices. I was handed three basals when I came on board. He was okay with my refusal to use the accompanying workbooks cover to cover, and my explanation of how I'd start using the basals as anthologies while easing in some student-selected and teacher-selected authentic literature. The contracting thing was kind of complex, so I thought I'd save it for later.

> Vignette: It was April. My principal appeared at the door of my "contracted" class about three minutes after we had started. He was wearing a crisp shirt and tie and white shoes. His clipboard was in hand for an unannounced observation (unaffectionately dubbed by the staff as "Pearl Harbors"). I saw him out of the corner of my eye—he was looking for me where he expected me to be: in the front of the classroom. Then he ventured into the classroom to see what was going on. He nearly tripped over several belly-flopped readers who didn't even look up as they remained glued to their trade books. He looked quizzically at a small group cutting up magazines in order to create collages that captured the lyrics of their favorite songs. He glanced at the interactions at the peer-editing table, as well as at Brett and Robert collaborating on construction of a crossword puzzle for the class, which consisted of their self-selected vocabulary from *White Fang*. I think he had trouble locating me

because I was sitting on the floor in the middle of the room with Aneesha, conferencing with her on her original short story. Finally he walked over to me and informed me that he'd "come back some time when I was teaching." I just smiled. The kids just kept right on working as he walked out. He was really big on "time on task," and he recognized that the kids were very on task, but that they were *different* tasks. He later became a convert, but only after he saw the quality of student work produced, as well as positive parent feedback. I had to educate him about the amount of time it took to respond to the students' products, in addition to the amount of preparation it took to structure contracting time.

But what really sold him occurred about a month or so later when ("bombs away!") he dropped in for another Pearl Harbor. This time he was on time, but I was not—I had an emergency phone call, and I was in the team room, indisposed, not knowing that he was waiting in my room. The students arrived with their contracting folders, took them out, went to the turn in stations, conferencing areas, etc. and totally managed themselves until I arrived, just in time for the first writing conference.

As I am a *whole-part-whole* learner and teacher, it makes sense for me to look broadly, then to delve into particulars. My basics are presented in this chapter. Many of the specifics presented here are for my seventh grade classes, but they were adapted over many years from other grade levels. Although Chapter 7 deals exclusively with adjustments and examples for younger children, seventh graders are right in the middle of the middle, so they're a good choice for the examples to be given for the bulk of this chapter.

Some Basics

In my middle school setting I teach five classes—this team of students rotates among the same teachers, who see about 25 to 28 students per class. Kids throughout the school are grouped by teams, but other than for occasional brief, special projects, team teaching is not common. I find ways, however, to reinforce content area skills and strategies by bringing social studies and science curriculum into my classroom. My five classes are on contracts for about one third of the year each. During contracting time, most of my students are largely self-directed, but provisions for direct instruction are included. During the other two thirds of the year classes are slightly more teacher centered. I have learned to stagger contracting time, in order to distribute the paper and response load. For example, I am careful to limit the number of classes on contracts and due dates are always a few days apart. Additionally, classroom rules are essentially congruent and consistent, as are my behavior and expectations, whether on or off contracts.

Additionally, my students are consistently involved in self-selected reading (SSR) and *journaling* throughout the year whether on or off contracts. Room arrangement is pretty much unchanged throughout the year (Figure 2–1). I do have the luxury of a large, carpeted room, with a panoramic view to boot. Students are used to having access to their own work, present and past, and move freely from the dump portfolios (stored in open crates) to their working portfolios, which contain their contracting works in progress. The dump portfolios are simply repositories for storage throughout the year, but they are fluid and useful when parts of them are used to build the working portfolios. As the contracting cycles draw to a close, the contents of the working contract then go to the dump (storage) folders, where they may lie fallow for several months or for the rest of the year, or they may be resurrected for the new contract learning cycle.

I never launch into contracting until at least a month of the school year has passed. September is always the time to establish expectations and a sense of interdependence and trust and safety. Key expectations are modeled and practiced

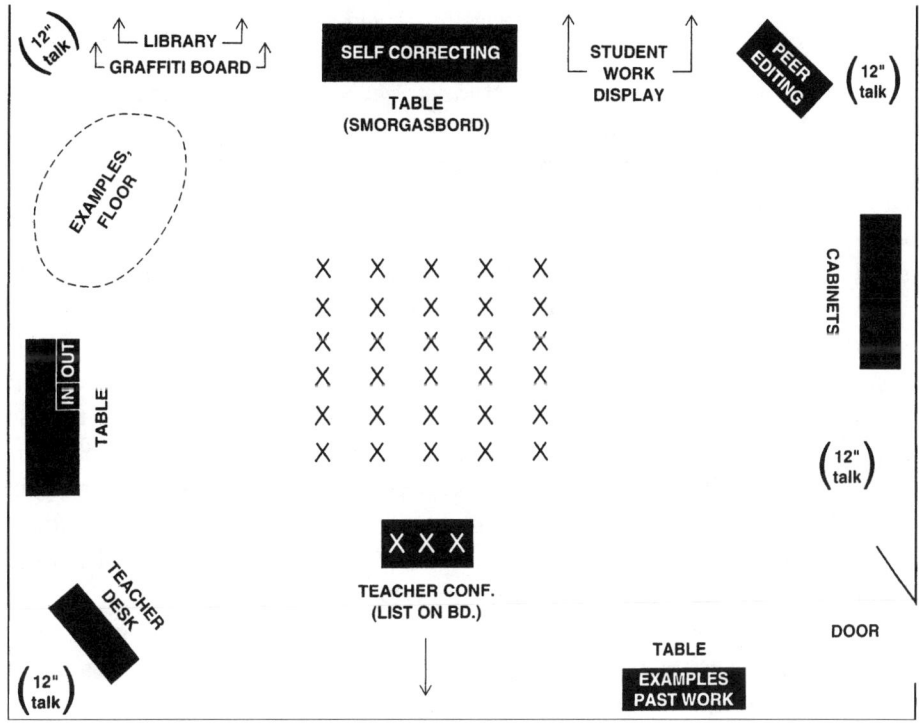

Figure 2–1. Room arrangement

explicitly: peer conferencing, positive feedback, pairing, and twelve-inch voices. I have learned over the years to do less content teaching early in the year in order to teach the community classroom skills that will enable more learning over the long haul. We take the time to use fishbowl techniques to model and role play and practice group skills, and I do a lot of thinking aloud, asking the students to do the same. *Twelve-inch voices* are absolutely essential for pairing and conferencing—students practice whispering to partners so that those (not quite literally) more than twelve inches away cannot hear them. We also practice the art of giving positive, yet honest feedback. Finally, we work on establishing automaticity through the use of nonverbal cues (hand signals to expedite routines, from bathroom usage to pencil sharpening).

A big dose of marketing and promoting doesn't hurt either, as contracting is alluded to in reverent terms as an upcoming opportunity, when they are ready, to show their emerging skills.

As the time for the first contract draws near, I spend a great deal of time in preparation. Adequate time to explain to students the rationale for using contracts is a must (the previously mentioned four recurring themes about middle schoolers and contracts on page 2 are well received and related to by my students) and specific behavioral and performance expectations are spelled out. At the onset of the contracting cycle each student receives necessary papers, guideline sheets and journal books, and the contract itself. The first contract (Contract 1, see Appendix, p. 100) typically spells out a variety of specific tasks to be completed, time allowances, and payoffs; students and I sign the document, and it is turned over to the student for safekeeping. The first contract of the year is fairly brief in duration, and largely nonnegotiable as opposed to the more flexible contracts planned for the future, but more on that later.

The next sample contract I have included (see Appendix, p. 101) is still quite structured because it is from relatively early in the year. The abbreviations used are meaningful to my students, as we balance district curricular mandates with more generative needs. As we gradually hone in on optimal use of time and resources, the students develop real-life work skills of time management and planning. They learn to deal with smaller, conscripted tasks as well as bigger, broader projects. Choices (some) are built in but are typically fairly minimal until students demonstrate their capacity to handle responsibility.

From the beginning of the year the classroom is arranged with designated peer pairing areas, self-correction stations, turn-in stations, editing areas, and a library, but contracting time is when it all gets used simultaneously. The students are permitted to do their assigned and self-selected tasks in any sequence, and at any reasonable location, just as long as the contract is completed satisfactorily by the agreed upon due date. The short first contract enables me to focus the students on clear goals and allows the children to reap immediate benefits such as prompt feedback, praise, feelings of success, and/or tangible rewards. I again need to stress that the first contract should be short. Depending on your comfort level and that of your students, about three days' duration should be good for the first time—but students and teachers vary. I usually make the first one a one week contract.

As the year progresses, more and more control is relinquished to the students. Contracts then become longer in duration and much more negotiable. Typically, these contracts spell out time and a few nonnegotiable (teacher selected) activities, but gradually include more negotiable (student selected) weight for items chosen from a menu (see Appendix, p. 102).

Many contract activities lend themselves to peer tutoring and cooperative activities, without *requiring* cooperation when individual styles, predilections, or simply the nature of the activity militate against forced cooperation. Most young adolescents love to interact with their peers, and it is possible to harness and direct these interactions. As opposed to the ubiquitous, structured, classical *cooperative learning,* I've found that pairs are optimal for contracting. My students negotiate for formal collaborative activities (e.g., coauthorship of a choose-your-own-adventure story; write and illustrate a fable to be read to younger children) or pair informally as needs arise. Partner work is typically done on the periphery of the classroom, with the central space reserved for all quiet work. To help ensure successful interactions among the pairs or groups while respecting the needs of those engaged in quiet activities, we (myself included, of course) are required to use the aforementioned twelve-inch voices for collaborative work. The students have invented a verb from this when asking for permission, as in "May I twelve-inch talk with Tyvon today? We need about half of the period to work on our word bank." Contracting is deceptively simple. The teacher takes chunks of content/strategies/process that need to be *covered* anyway. He or she then sets parameters for students to incrementally take control of time and process, and, eventually, make choices as to products and demonstrations.

Middle schoolers, in addition to exercising freedom of control by negotiating for projects and activities, very much enjoy the freedom of control of their learning environments (where, when, and with whom). Some are simply happy to be trusted to move, to ensconce themselves in a secluded corner to work quietly, or to belly flop on the carpeted floor. All of this contributes to a sense of ownership. As one of my students stated on her end of contract evaluation, "Your class is really fun. We don't have to be planted in the seats all the time. I like the way you let us move around."

Conferencing

Contracts provide opportunities for the personalization that is so sorely lacking in many traditional classrooms. Contracts provide the teacher and student or groups of students with an opportunity to communicate both in writing (via journals) and orally (through conferences). For schools without an advisory program, the conference time enhances the adult–student linkage, which is often missing for middle level youth.

One form of conferencing, which young people really relish, is the negotiating session. When contracts are partially or largely negotiable, students should be provided with a variety of means to attain the required content (reading, research, media, peer interaction) as well as alternative methods for demonstrating what they have learned. The menu from which my students select their negotiables (see Appendix 103) is essentially a compendium of student-suggested projects that I complied over several years. A good deal more on the art of negotiation is included in following chapters, but a quick discussion follows.

More on Negotiation

The following three questions are critical for all learning and for contracting in particular.

- What do students need to know?
- What do students want to know?
- What do students already know?

The need-to-know question is defined by the curriculum, the community, and the teacher. The teacher does not abdicate the responsibility to teach important skills, strategies, and content during contract time; far from it. If, for example, the district or state standard/expectation is that students use direct quotes appropriately and accurately, the teacher sees that the job gets done. It's simply easier to teach such a skill in an authentic setting with a real purpose. It is also instructionally sound to provide the needed direct instruction to the targeted audience only, without worrying about managing the remainder of the class. The other students have plenty to do, and the teacher is free to focus full attention on those in need.

The already-know question is important as well. When a seventh grader comes to me as a skilled and motivated writer who is secure in (and bored by) writing a one-paragraph expository theme with three supporting details and a clincher, it is my call (and hers) to move along the continuum and seek greater challenges.

The want-to-know question is most important. Using the menu as a spring-board, students can propose motivating and meaningful activities. Again, more specifics on negotiating are coming, but kids truly relish choices and work hard to showcase their skills. The wise teacher takes in all of this information and more in nudging, cajoling, and guiding student choices. In Karen Grimm's present sixth grade classes, she has double blocks of reading/language arts time provided in her six, seven, and eight middle school schedule. Karen capitalized on the film versions of Harry Potter and the Tolkien trilogy and had many students read the books and view the movies and compare and contrast—gladly and enthusiastically. Marc, on the other hand, was a former student of mine who got very interested in Marco Polo after watching a miniseries on television. He negotiated to write a report on Polo and to give an oral presentation to the class. He chose to read a pretty scholarly biography on the explorer. Negotiations and counter negotiations are meaningful for my students as suggestions and proposals take shape and evolve.

Remember to guide your students in their making choices. Be aware, as well, that honoring student wishes and initiatives is not embraced by all teachers. Recently, one of my colleagues (who happens to be an eighth grade reading teacher) challenged the notion of empowerment and choice for kids. He went on a mini-tirade, complaining:

"Life is not about choices in the real world. Kids will face jobs where 'whatever floats your boat' is just not acceptable. Their employers are not going to give them choices about whether to do a job or not!"

My partial answer to the colleague was that my students, present and past, do not have the option to do (or not do) their jobs. They do, however, do their jobs better when they have choice and options about their work.

Skill Work and Self-Corrections

Workbook activities are the bane of most middle schoolers' academic lives. Even when curriculum supervisors cut back workbooks, teachers respond by creating *packets,* which are often just as onerous. (As you learn to trust yourself while breaking away from decontextualized skill work that may be required of you in the name of *accountability,* it is important to empower the students as much as possible.) Under contracts, skill work is more palatable for students when they score for themselves the type of work that has publisher-made or teacher-made answer keys. This, of course, frees the teacher for more important tasks such as individual student conferences and small group skill reinforcement or enrichment instruction. When a self-correction station, replete with answer keys and colored pencils, is set up in the classroom and rules are established and clearly explained so that students take their responsibilities seriously, they are much more involved in thoughtfully analyzing answers ("Do I give myself half or full credit for this one? I had something different than the answer key, but I think it means about the same thing.") than when the teacher does all of the correcting. By placing the students in control, the contract helps alter their perceptions about skill activities. Some actually enjoy skill work for a change. Once again, students feel a sense of power and ownership regarding their learning.

Journals

Learning contracts should include components that allow students to react to their experiences and to enter into discourse about learning and life with their teacher and with each other. Beane (1990) discussed the personal concerns of early adolescents as they struggle to understand the particular stage they are in and to deal with the change it involves. A dialogue journal is an effective conduit for establishing this communication linkage with middle level students. Journaling activities provide an integrated approach to the contract that fosters a real context in which students can practice written skills and can communicate their excitement (or frustrations) regarding specific topics, from home life to peer pressure to their progress on the contract itself. Of course, emphasis is placed on the communication aspect of writing and not on the mechanics as the students concentrate on reflection and personal meaning. Under contracts, I use a two-sided format in which half of the journal book is dialogue, where they may write about any topic and receive teacher or peer response. The other half of the contracting journal book is reserved for a learning log, where they are limited to addressing specific questions raised in their contract studies. As an example, one of my past students had negotiated to read *Gone with the Wind*, rent the movie version, and write a paper comparing and contrasting the two treatments. Additionally, as she read the novel, she jotted down reflections, comments, and questions that she shared with me along the way as she saw fit. In another case, a student who was reading *The Red Badge of Courage* negotiated to describe the feelings of a thirteen-year-old boy living in Gettysburg and to relate them to feelings that he may have had if he were involved in a threatening situation. Tasks such as these require students to gather information, metacogitate and gather their thoughts, and develop a response. Learning logs are particularly useful for interdisciplinary contracts, for they can be shared by participating teachers.

Readings

Learning contracts provide the perfect platform for involving students in real reading that extends beyond typical schooling and required, traditional texts.

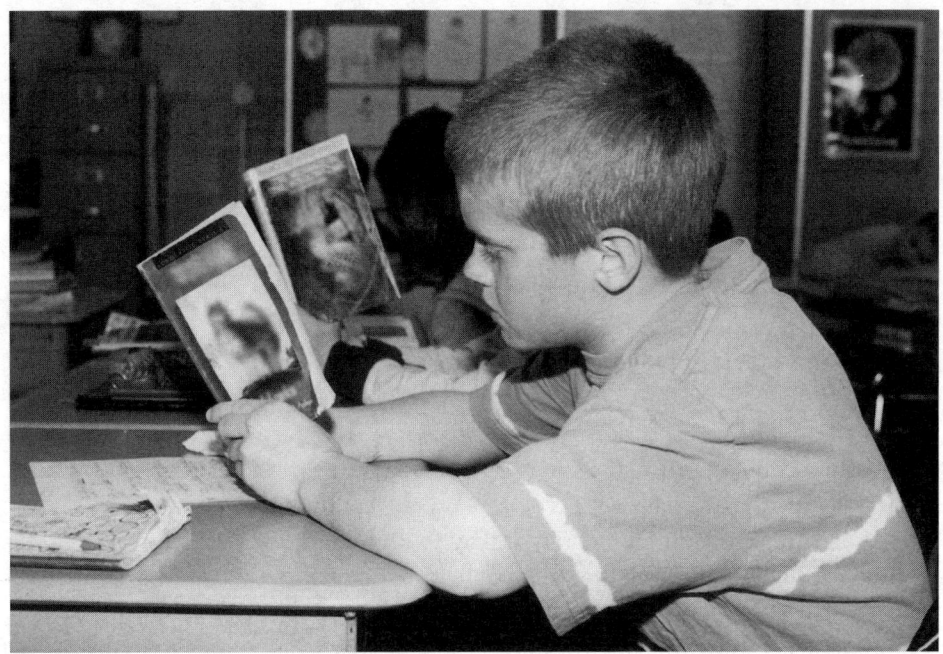

In direct contrast to the sometimes damning data about how little our young adolescents value and practice independent reading, I have found that many of them can be voracious consumers of books when they are provided with the proper balance of choice, guidance, and encouragement. Each of my contracts includes the reading of at least one student-selected book; their method of response to the book, whether written, oral, by conferencing/interest group, or other is of course negotiable. Recommendations that are personalized, from teachers or from peers, are well received; this is a trendy age, and serial books are very popular, but I have found that my students over the years have been willing to tackle Jack London and Sir Arthur Conan Doyle in addition to V. C. Andrews and Christopher Pike. The project that entails the comparison of a book with its movie version (Greenwood 1989) is particularly popular, as the students avidly read a wide range of good literature.

As with the learning logs, reading under contract parameters involves my students in holistic, interdisciplinary learning that good middle level schools are supposed to foster. For example, while doing interdisciplinary contracts in language arts and social studies classes, students can be reading a host of historical fiction books that dovetail with content for both contracts. In another case, a physical education teacher, a science teacher, and an advisory group leader might work together to have students read and discuss Judy Blume's *Blubber*. This would provide a means of establishing a cross-curricular thematic-based unit focused on the physical development needs of their students.

Exhibitions

At the completion of a particular contract cycle, the students may opt to demonstrate what they have learned in a variety of ways, depending on what is negotiated for. An exhibition of what the student has learned can and should take many forms. A student might prepare a written paper of publishable quality, make an oral presentation to a small or large group, teach a class, make use of media, or produce a working model. The key, again, is for the teacher to relinquish control to the students, in this case to give them some say over how they will show what they have learned. Demonstrating what has been learned in a variety of ways encourages creativity in the classroom and improves self-worth and competence. In short, the student "learns to win recognition by producing things" (Erikson 1963, 259).

Tips on Contract Setup

More specifics follow, but at this juncture I pause and attempt to synthesize some key reminders, based on years of experience and experimentation and tinkering, regarding the use of learning contracts. Remember my whole-part-whole predilections!

- Start slowly in terms of time, volume of work, and negotiability of early contracts
- Explicitly teach the necessary procedures and social skills
- Arrange the classroom thoughtfully
- Establish a comfortable (accepting yet challenging) climate
- Avoid emphasis on product to the exclusion of process
- Display current and past student work
- Give prompt teacher feedback; allow and encourage peer feedback
- Involve students in self-assessment
- Experiment, take risks, and listen to kids
- Respect and enjoy kids

Several of the points mentioned previously need more emphasis. I find it essential to provide *exemplars* (samples) of past work. As when we share anchors with students in advance to make a rubric more meaningful, there is a risk of overimitation and lack of originality when past products are displayed. But I've found that the advantages far outweigh the disadvantages. The exemplars I choose make the rubrics such as the one in the Appendix (see p. 103) come alive, for my students are able to see what quality work looks like, which takes them

beyond reading descriptions about what constitutes good work. The upside is increased comfort and a determination to equal or exceed the quality of the work displayed. It is also important to actively involve students in rubric development. I typically take a sample product or performance and work with students in teasing out criteria and describing them. Remember to always get student permission and to preserve anonymity when appropriate. The combination of exemplar and rubric is absolutely critical to the production of quality work.

Prompt and thoughtful teacher *feedback* is valued so much by children. It is a real mistake to not distribute pupils' work. If you refer again to the room arrangement floor plan (see Figure 2–1), the turn-in station is critical. My kids are taught to move freely to the in/out boxes, and they drop finished products in the box and don't have to wait until the end of the contract period for teacher reaction.

I cannot stress enough how much students value prompt, specific feedback. This is also a real help to me in distributing my response load, for I will have seen and responded to the bulk of each student's work before final turn-in time.

As students try to work through the necessary crisis of adolescence they need and want teachers who care about them personally and who convey respect and trust in their capabilities as learners. These young people need to understand the reasons for acquiring specific skills and information, and they need to feel in control of their lives. The activities associated with learning contracts provide a vehicle to permit the connection between previously isolated content areas and the personal interests and needs of the student. The contract allows students some say in what and how they will learn and still allows the teacher to maintain control while segueing into the role of facilitator and enabler. Most important, contracting establishes a climate in the classroom that clearly signals that students are valued, respected, and capable of assuming responsibility for a large portion of their learning. What better way is there to set the tone for life-long learning?

Sample Schedules

In an elementary, self-contained setup, the teacher has plenty of control over how time is spent. Contracting teachers I've worked with typically set aside their entire language arts blocks. Jeff Singleton, for example, might dedicate Monday, Wednesday, and Friday for ninety minutes each day for two weeks to contracting, depending on the time of year and his students' instructional needs.

In my present middle school setting, sixth grade has a double block of language arts, and the teacher sees fewer children over the course of the year than in seventh or eighth grade. Karen Grimm is able to use her 8:40 to 10:20 block or her 12:30 to 2:10 block without overlap; additionally, she builds in daily whole-class minilessons.

In seventh grade, we are on a six-day cycle and I work with fifty-minute periods. Whereas Linda Rief (Kaufman 2001) takes ten minutes for the minilesson and ten minutes for sharing in her daily fifty-minute workshops (leaving thirty student-controlled minutes), I give my kids forty plus minutes daily to be self-directed while they are on contracts, with three to five minutes of teacher time at each end of the period.

Figures 2–2 and 2–3 help to spell this out; they show a weekly schedule and my annual calendar/timeline.

In the week in late October, only two of my five classes, a total of fifty-two children, are on contracts. This early contract lasts fifteen school days, approximately three weeks, depending on holidays. I stagger the turn-in days, so that I only get about half of the completed contract sets on a Friday, the rest on Monday. As the first two classes go off contract, the next two are about to go on.

Week of October 24–28			Day 3	Day 4	Day 5	Day 6	Day 1
			Monday	Tuesday	Wednesday	Thursday	Friday
Advisory	Advisory	8:20–8:40					
Period 1	7-0	8:40–9:30	contracting	contracting	contracting	contracting	contracting
Period 2	7-P	9:30–10:20	contracting	contracting	contracting	contracting	contracting
Period 3	Team Planning/ Prep	10:20–11:30					
Period 4	7-W	11:10–11:30 12:00–12:30	JGB	P4C	P4C	Persuasive	Persuasive
Period 5	7-R	12:30–1:20	JGB	P4C	P4C	Persuasive	Persuasive
Period 6	7-Y	1:20–2:10	JGB	P4C	P4C	Expository	Expository
Period 7	Specials	2:10–3:00					

Figure 2–2. Sample seventh grade weekly schedule

Time Line						School Year _____ to _____			
Sept	Oct	Nov	Dec	Jan	Feb	Mar	Apr	May	June
7-0	5 15	15 15 x	x x	20 20 20 20		25 25	25 25 25		
7-P	5 15	15 15 x	x x	20 20 20 20		25 25	25 25 25		
7-W	5	15 x	15 15 x x		20 20 20 20			25 25 25 25	25
7-R	5	15 x	15 15 x x		20 20 20 20			25 25 25 25	25
7-4	5	15 x	15 15 x x		20 20	20 20		25 25 25 25	25

Key: x = holiday; 5 = one-week contract; 15 = three-week contract; 20 = four-week contract; 25 = five-week contract.

Figure 2–3. Sample seventh grade yearly schedule highlighting contract cycles

In the year, each section is on contract for a total of sixty-five school days, fifty minutes a day. There are several weeks when a third class is on at the same time, but these are kept minimal. If you refer to 7-O and 7-P from Figure 2–2, the weekly schedule, both were on contract for one week in early October (five days) and now they are on contract for three weeks, the last week in October and the first two weeks in November, for a total of fifteen school days. The sections go off of their contracting cycles until January, when they do a four-week contract (designated as 20); then their final contracting time will be five weeks in duration, spanning late March and into May. I choose, for continuity purposes, to schedule contracting time for consecutive days in a full block, but it is possible to schedule your own contracting for designated days of the week or cycle.

Contracts can also overlap and support other learning strategies and structures such as centers, readers'/writers' workshops, and literature circles. They also complement any direct instruction time when the teacher needs to focus on an individual or a flexible group. In Karen Grimm's aforementioned double blocks with her sixth graders, she can rotate these groups of six students each into literature circles while the remaining students do paired or individual contract time. This affords her the opportunity to do a little extra assessment of targeted kids or just to pay closer attention to the discussion groups, while the other students self-manage with meaningful work that they have chosen. This requires good record keeping, of course. But the payoff is obvious, particularly in the variety afforded to the children.

What It All Looks Like

In one of my normal fifty-minute periods, my seventh graders enter the room with contracting portfolios. Most go straight to their regular desks, open folders, and get to work. Some go directly to the aforementioned in/out boxes and others to the board to sign up for conferences. Groups (typically pairs) that want permission to work together raise their hands or gesture to me. Some of the children often like to concentrate on one task for the period, although others break up the period–possibly spending twenty minutes or so reading their self-selected books, then doing some journaling.

I'll interrupt briefly to make announcements, but I try to keep such interruptions to a minimum. Flexible skill groups meet periodically to address specific needs, then disband. Advance notice is given for scheduled oral presentations, so that children can plan their time. There is plenty of movement, but it is purposeful. Kids move freely back and forth to in/out boxes, to me, to the library, and to the reference area. Quiet abounds for the most part, and whatever talk that does occur is purposeful and structured.

The last three minutes are Q & A time. I answer general, public questions, and do a lot of thinking aloud. We often use this time for crossword seminar when they ask publicly for help with their above-grade level challenge puzzles. Some students opt to keep right on working independently until it's time for dismissal.

Vignette: One of my classes of seventh graders is working on contracts. It is fifth period, right before lunch. With five minutes to go, I give the signal to return to their seats for a status of the class and general announcements. Chris has been sitting at his desk, obviously immersed in his self-selected reading. He doesn't take his nose out of his book as his compatriots gather up their stuff and return to their seats. There's some general chatter, and I answer questions. On this day I dismiss by footwear. "All Reeboks may go to lunch . . . all Nikes . . . all K Swiss. . . ." The kids rumble down the aisles cheerfully. I notice that Chris's nose is still in the book. I finally say "Anybody else—the rest of you may go." Nose still in book. Remember, twelve years old, lunchtime. I decide that Chris is putting me on, just the two of us in the room now. I decide that I'll wait him out, so I go about responding to some journals, go over my plans. I glance at him occasionally—nose still in book. Fifteen minutes pass. It's very quiet; the yelling in the halls and the slamming of locker doors have subsided since all the kids are in the cafeteria at the other end of the building. I finally walk over to him and put a hand on his shoulder. He jumps a bit, looks up at me with startled blue eyes, like Snow White or Rip Van Winkle coming back from far away. I say, "Chris, don't you want to go to lunch?" He looks around and realizes the room is empty. He is genuinely surprised. He says, simply, "I was at a really good part. . . ."

3

Turning Them Loose

Teaching is consuming work—time consuming, energy consuming, and self consuming. When we stop long enough to have conversations, those of us who teach lament that we have "no life." Teaching leaves us spent, fragile, and tired. We long for time to organize ourselves, to slow down and think deeply. If we stay in teaching long, it's because we learn to rejuvenate ourselves and to put things in our own lives into perspective. We use the lessons we've learned in life to make sense of the work.

—B. BERGHOFF
Language Arts, September 1997

We've covered the rationale and philosophy, as well as the basics of contracting. You as a reader should understand the rudiments of gradually relinquishing control to students. In this chapter I delve a little deeper into the art of negotiation and establishing parameters to ensure quality work. I also give more detail on selected menu choices.

As I give details about nonnegotiable and negotiable projects that are built into my contracts, I want to emphasize that they are not sacrosanct—they are simply the things that work for my kids in this context. The things that my kids do are not necessarily innovative, and there is no recipe for success with contracting. What matters is the balance of teacher guidance and student initiative, the customization. Students typically know what they want and know what they need—it's just that teachers don't often ask.

I teach about 130 middle school kids a year, ranging (of course) in abilities, tastes, and motivation. The nonnegotiable sections of their contracts are essentially the same, but even that portion is flexible. What truly differentiates is the negotiable part. Some students are broad and thematic, some are browsers in what

they undertake. It is up to me, however, to nudge gently (or be directive) in steering students toward good choices.

The astute teacher discerns how the students function under the terms of the early, structured contracts, paying attention to both product and process. Here the Tomlinson continuum is very useful (see Figure 1–1). I actually use Dr. Tomlinson's tool with my kids in conferring and goal setting—with some I do blind review, with each of us assessing the child's performance. Here are two important points to remember:

- In my experience, many teachers of the gifted/talented/motivated student tend to differentiate quantitatively as opposed to qualitatively. That is, they assign *more*. This is not fair to kids. Contracts allow for appropriate customization.
- Children tend to overchallenge themselves more often than they underchallenge. I find that I must take things off of their plates more often than not. I allow a window of time for renegotiation, and they can always do extra credit if they finish early.

Products from the Menu

Developmental differences from fourth to ninth grade (in the case of this book) can be easily met with a modicum of common sense and a bit of tinkering and a willingness to be flexible. Younger children generally need just a bit more scaffolding and structure and shorter time spans in the early stages, as outlined in Chapter 7.

As teachers listen to kids, they see the purpose of contracts as much more than keeping them busy. Through examples, reflection, and feedback, students really focus on producing quality work. Please refer back to the menu of seventh grade negotiables (see Appendix, p. 102) as you read the following section.

Linchpin: The Summary and Critique and Hybrids (Menus 1, 2, 3, and 4)

During the first month of school before contracting startup, I model and the students practice summarizing and critiquing. We practice on magazine articles, movies, and books. I do not use the first person pronoun in a summary, but often in a critique I do. Guideline sheets are provided and kept throughout the year for easy referral. This is where the previously mentioned dump portfolios are useful. As I mentioned in Chapter 2, a true portfolio involves reflection and self-evaluation. The dump portfolios are used strategically at times, but are essentially for storage.

The summary and critique (see Appendix, p. 104), and its hybrids, are then options for response to a book or some other text. Response is negotiable—it might be in the form of a series of journal entries or an exit conference with a peer or the teacher. But the summary and critique is a staple from which students choose to depart.

A particularly rich activity is the book and movie project: summary, compare, contrast, and critique. I attempt, when feasible, to harness and capitalize on the interest of the students when it comes to viewing and visually representing the newer language arts enumerated in the National Council of Teachers of English/International Reading Association (NCTE/IRA) standards. The competition for students' time is fierce. Parents and teachers bemoan the problems presented by our video age; it is said that children watch too much television. Teachers' attempts at accountability of self-selected student reading (e.g., book reports) are sometimes thwarted and often resented as unmotivating by students. The format of the movie paper is quite similar to that of the book summary and critique. The critique, however, includes discussion of the appropriateness of the Motion Picture Association of America (MPAA) rating (if available) of the film. Later in the year I assign the summary, compare, contrast, and critique paper. An assignment such as this does not, of course, have to be done under learning contract parameters, but teachers must make provisions for ample time. It does not matter whether movie viewing precedes book reading or vice versa, as long as both steps are done carefully and thoughtfully. I always provide samples of past students' works and a guideline sheet that clearly delineates the separate parts of the paper (see Appendix, page 104).

Heading. For clarity and brevity, students simply list the following information:

    A. Title
    B. Author of book
    C. Time and setting (of both book and movie)
    D. Main characters (of both book and movie)
    E. MPAA rating of movie (if available)

Summary. Students are required to limit their summaries to two or three paragraphs, maximum. I remind them repeatedly that Oscar Wilde once apologized for writing a long letter because he did not have time to write a short one. They are taught to focus on the essential action of the book and movie. Any differences in treatment of book and movie are not to be dealt with in this section of the paper. Here, the early direct instruction, modeling, and sharing from September begin to pay their dividends. I term it *front loading*: Careful, extensive time is spent early on to save time later and to enable divergent activities and projects later in the year.

Compare. This section is typically quite brief. The students are simply asked to recount the major similarities between the book and movie versions. They learn to focus on the big picture, without dwelling on small details.

Contrast. As opposed to the compare section, this segment can become quite lengthy, depending on the book and movie chosen. For example, several years ago one of my ninth grade students found major changes in Hollywood's treatment of Stephen King's *Christine.* She recognized that key characters and events in the book were entirely omitted in the movie version, for instance. She also found that the movie version added minor characters and plot developments. The contrast section often gives a clear indication of how carefully the students have read. I urge them not to get hung up on every minute difference; rather, the students are instructed to deal with global differences and a few concrete examples of these. Typically, students come to realize that authors have greater latitude to delve into detail and description than do screenwriters.

Critique. This is the crucial segment of the paper. As in their prior book-only critique, they provide a recommendation; as in their prior movie-only critique, they deal with the appropriateness of the MPAA rating. Additionally, they are required to tell whether they enjoyed the film or the book better, and why. I am pleased to report that my students overwhelmingly prefer books over movies.

Some teachers may want to place limits on what is commonly thought to be objectionable material. My policy is to defer the final decision as to what is or is not appropriate to the parents of my students as well as the students themselves. I do reserve the right to approve or disapprove my students' selections; they are well aware of my distaste for what I term "slice and dice" movies. In short, I try to be reasonable in steering them toward books and movies with at least some artistic merit.

As early adolescents move from concrete to formal operations, they certainly are capable of mulling over and analyzing censorship and taste issues. Children who are notorious for being self-centered become very aware of others' perspectives and tastes when they have an authentic reason for doing so. I always find it best to be proactive and candid with them. I involve them in understanding that what is objectionable to one individual is not necessarily so to another—whether it be a book, a film, or some other medium. We talk about how being *exposed* to something objectionable does not mean that we will emulate it. We talk about respect for the rights of others balanced with the mores and expectations of schools and schooling. I stress the difference between self-selected assignments versus required, whole-class selections. We have decided together over the years that censorship, quality, and taste issues are serious business.

When the students discuss the MPAA rating of a film, I expect them to discern whether a particular rating is due to language, violence, adult situations (this also presents an opportunity for an auxiliary lesson that seizes a *teachable moment* on euphemisms) or some other criterion. Obviously, this can be a sensitive issue, but if parents are communicated with and students are treated in an appropriate manner, the likelihood of problems is minimal. Being proactive about book selection is of paramount importance; see the sample parent letter for a model (see Appendix, p. 106).

I conduct periodic temperature checks of my courses, as well as more formalized anonymous evaluations at the end of each semester. My students have indicated repeatedly that the book-to-movie comparison activity is an overwhelming favorite. When provided with time and encouragement, their products have been astonishingly good. Self-selection, of course, is the key. In the past years, for example, my seventh graders read such challenging books as *Gone with the Wind*, *The African Queen*, *The Old Man and the Sea*, and *Lord of the Flies* so that they could compare them with their movie versions. Perhaps my favorite comment was contained in the critique of a twelve-year-old boy who said that he preferred the novel *Treasure Island* to its movie counterpart, because "the movie was in black and white, and my imagination is in color."

For book selection, I am constantly wrestling with the *quality* issue. My students are required to have a book *in process* all the time, whether contracting or not. I want them to be engaged and to be devouring print. Some years ago I needed to find a way to balance their engagement with their parents' wishes, for parents often want Skippy reading *Robinson Crusoe* as opposed to a biography of David Robinson. I solved the quality issue with what we call "the shopping list," a recommended reading list of classics and neo-classics. I periodically stipulate that their self-selected reading books have to be from the preapproved list. The kids are fine with the notion of mixing choices, and they have come to discover some good literature that they might have not otherwise been drawn to. Additionally, I have been able to build a serviceable classroom library largely on extra credit donations, by sending a plea to parents via their kids. A lot of used books are shelved in homes and simply needed to be redistributed. It has been a real pleasure to see our classroom library grow. Great books that would eventually go to garage sales or the dumpster get recycled in a different, richer way.

You may wish to see Kaufman (2001) for a thorough discussion as to how Linda Rief manages and organizes her classroom library. I am admittedly less meticulous than she is—I suspect that many of the donated books have been lost along the way. But I'm guessing that many have found new homes and are being read again and again.

Vocabulary/Word Study Choices (Menus 5, 6, 7, 18, and 19)

Early adolescents are perfectly capable of discerning what vocabulary is new and interesting to them. A large wall of my room is covered with butcher paper and dubbed the graffiti board. Students are invited to come forward and contribute their favorite words, poems, quotes, pictures, and so forth. They also keep bookmarks with their self-selected books that have vocabulary expectations that need to be met.

My kids see crossword puzzles as grown up and fairly authentic. They are typically assigned a nonnegotiable packet of four or five and can negotiate to complete three or four more sets if they so choose, depending on contract length. They are particularly eager to go beyond grade level. Another popular menu choice is to create their own crosswords—typically around a theme or title. They then proudly offer their puzzles to their peers to solve, for credit or extra credit. This also sparks interest in the books from which the words were derived. I am a little less keen on the word search option, but it gets kids to be word detectives and it forces them to attend closely to grouping of new words as well as proper spelling. And in both cases, it is gratifying to see children voluntarily go to thesauri and dictionaries. The word bank is usually combined with the word search. The genesis of both is the simple bookmark; we use construction paper, cut in 4 × 11 inch strips. The children are taught to note new or interesting words by marking them lightly in pencil in the margins of their texts. They go back later and copy their words down in context using ellipses, so as only to have the essence of the meaning supplied by the surrounding words. They then locate an appropriate dictionary definition. Words are accumulated, and then shared in a variety of ways, from a word bank to a crossword puzzle to a word search to a word wall. Again, the personalization and the sharing of their *own* words is what really motivates them to become word detectives.

Analogies. I do a lot of work with my kids on analogies. They are typically assigned a packet that I put together, but they can negotiate to do extra packets or to create their own. Analogies are particularly useful for making interdisciplinary connections.

Retention is limited when formal vocabulary exercises dealing with disparate bits of information (e.g., word lists, study of word parts, synonyms, antonyms, and so forth) are employed. As an example, a worksheet (produced by the publisher of a sixth grade level basal text) defined the word *amateur* as "one who does something unskillfully." The follow-through activities supplied by the unknown author then reinforced that one shade of meaning of the word, expected the pupils to use the word in an original sentence, and so forth. Mary Lou Retton was an *amateur* in the Los Angeles Olympics, but few would classify her performance as unskillful. Such superficial, inflexible definitions often serve only to confuse young readers in transition.

Enhancing vocabulary enrichment through the use of analogical reasoning is preferable. Analogies involve the analysis of the correspondence among things that otherwise might be construed as dissimilar, for example: *silencer* is to *gun* as *muffler* is to *car*. Analogies are ideal for vocabulary development because they carry a built-in context, which demands some mental gymnastics on the part of the learner. Additionally, they are enjoyable for children to solve, create, and explain. The learner is required to discern shades of meaning, to be creative, to be flexible, and to attach experience to the words of others.

After a focus lesson or two on analogy creation and solution strategies, I assign packets with analogies such as these:

tire : rubber : : windshield : _____	angry : furious : : large : _____
Sue : _____ : : Bill : William	ten :_____ : : dime : dollar
cold : freezing : : _____ : _____	Romeo : Juliet : : _____ : _____

I prefer that these analogies *not* be multiple choice (which is a departure from the way analogies are typically tested), for in this way spelling skills are reinforced. Exceptions are made, however, for confused pairs, for example:

blew : blue : : threw : _____
(though, thought, through, trough)

Here, especially for weaker readers, choices are quite helpful.

Finally, the students create their own analogies, which they share. How far they go is again negotiable, and the discussions and explanations that ensue are often enlightening. A twelve-year-old former student developed and shared the following very original analogy: "man : dog : : girl : diamonds." This created some confusion among her classmates until she proudly explained that she had tapped the *best friend* cliché. It must be stressed that students enlarge their concept development and flexibility by listening to their peers explain their thoughts. It is the task of the teacher to set the stage for divergent answers and to encourage thoughtful discussion.

After analogies have been thoroughly introduced, they may then be extended to reinforce vocabulary and concepts in the content area subjects. Once the children have received a solid foundation in analogical reasoning and have gotten plenty of practice in application, they delight in creating cross-curricular analogies for their teachers and classmates to solve.

There are some limitations in language arts and mathematics, particularly math in which the students are not introduced to as much new vocabulary per se. Some student-generated analogies, all related to English and mathematics, follow. They were all created by seventh graders.

uni : _____ : : tri : quad   228 : 12 : : 361 : _____
625 : _____ : : 25 : 5 $^3/_4$: .75 : : _____ : .875
perimeter : _____ : : area : interior   L'Amour : Sackett : : _____ : Finn
noun : adjective : : verb : _____   Holmes : _____ : : Batman : Robin
_____ : poetry : : paragraph : prose   isn't : _____ : : you : y'all

The greatest opportunities for vocabulary reinforcement are found in science and social studies, in which many new terms are introduced daily by content teachers. When I ask my kids to create science and social studies analogies, they are encouraged to make use of their text books, class notes, maps, current events handouts, and the like. For example, I might require them to create ten each in science and social studies as a nonnegotiable item. Next, I categorize and compile and redistribute these analogies for the entire class to solve and discuss. Some student-generated examples (this time with answers included) follow:

Social Studies
Mt. St. Helen's : Washington : : Mt. Hood : Oregon
USSR : bear : : USA : eagle
latitude : horizontal : : longitude : vertical
isthmus : land : : strait : water
consumer : buyer : : retailer : seller

Marcos : Philippines : : Duvalier : Haiti
San Francisco : trolley : : Venice : gondola
Aztecs : Mexico : : Incas : Peru
Dismal : Virginia : : Okeefenokee : Georgia

Science

anterior : posterior : : dorsal : ventral
sponge : porifera : : hydra : coelenterate
Darwin : evolution : : Einstein : relativity
intestines : digestive : : veins : circulatory
tapeworm : parasitic : : pilot fish : symbiotic
nucleus : nuclei : : flagellum : flagella
cheetah : carnivorous : : deer : herbivorous
seal : pup : : kangaroo : joey
bread : mold : : metal : rust
tadpole : frog : : caterpillar : butterfly
zoology : animals : : botany : plants

In the absence of true team teaching, as I mentioned earlier, this allows me to help reinforce necessary vocabulary for content area learning.

The examples given here have included all four parts of the analogy. Of course, when the teacher-compiled handout is distributed to the students, one word is omitted in varying places in the analogy. For variety, sometimes only the stem is given, with both parts of the answer provided by the student. My kids have no problem with the inclusion of proper nouns in the analogies, although purists might not consider proper nouns to be vocabulary per se.

We've also played with other content areas such as music and foreign language:

cymbal : percussion : : trombone : brass
girl : fille : : boy : garçon

These are just some possibilities, depending on the energy and ambition of students and teachers.

Journaling (Menu 10)

Students are subjected to so many *on-demand* writing tasks in school. For journaling under contract, my students choose the most comfortable and productive time and place for writing. We have gradually settled on a system of journal writing on a page-quota basis, without a time requirement. My kids, for the most part, love journaling because they get a response. I have never been totally happy with the page-quota arrangement, for it is so blatantly quantitative—but it has permitted us to get to the qualitative issues that truly matter.

Included in the learning contract packages that my students receive is a twenty-four-page composition notebook. As mentioned earlier, the notebook is two sided: one section is the dialogue journal, whereas the other is reserved for learning logs. For their first extended contract period, after the initial, brief one-week contract in early October, I typically require in addition to other activities, a specific number of pages of writing over a three-week period, although many children choose to do much more. They write in class, at lunch, on the bus, on the plane en route to a family vacation, in the car, or (usually) in the peace and quiet of their own homes. Several other procedures also promote journal writing:

- I distribute a few student journals from past years as samples. Names are removed and permission has been secured from the authors. This modeling by former students, which includes samples of my responses, helps provide initial structure and guidelines.
- I give them a firm commitment of confidentiality, promising never to share their thoughts with anyone without seeking their permission first. The samples here were excerpted with my students' permission.
- A procedure for the use of *graded* and *ungraded* turn-in boxes is established. As mentioned in Chapter 2 (you may wish to see the floor plan as well) these in/out boxes are very important. Kids value feedback on all of their work, but particularly regarding their journals. Students drop in unread journal entries at any time and receive the promise that their writings will be read on the spot if possible and definitely responded to by the next school day.
- Students write about a wide array of topics. I do make it clear, however, that "breakfast-to-bed" entries ("I had juice and Frosted Flakes. I almost missed the bus. We got lots of homework in math class. . . .") are boring and are to be avoided.

Importance of Teacher Response. The teachers of early adolescents are a special breed, as captured in Figure 3–1. These qualities are easy to enumerate, but difficult to practice. The characteristics in the figure are particularly useful when considering the power of thoughtful and targeted teacher response to what students write. Thoughtful teachers must be nonjudgmental and absolutely must resist the temptation to red-ink errors. It is essential that responses be directed toward content. I briefly compliment my writers on effective word choice (particularly risk taking in using new vocabulary), insightful observations, use of dialogue, and on communication that is lively and entertaining. A gradual relationship of trust usually develops. My children feel free to communicate with an adult who listens, gives advice when asked, and does not judge. As one of my students said:

Thanks for listening to my problem. I decided to stay living with my Dad. It was just good to be able to get it out. I know you're still my teacher, but when we do journals it's like you're more like a friend. It's sorta like there are different levels.

In this example, the student internalized a novel situation and expressed it. She stated something that peer pressure would not allow in most classroom (or interpersonal) discussions. Because peer approval is crucial to most middle-school-aged students, it constantly affects the quality of student–teacher interactions.

Cautions and Reservations. Although many teachers are understandably concerned about the time required to read and respond to student journals, I do not find this to be a problem. First of all, teachers can read student journals in a faster gear than other student products because their purpose is to read for content, not to correct. Second, the terms of a learning contract can distribute student work so that products are turned in at varying times. In this way the teacher has ample time to keep abreast of the writing and make timely comments. Finally, the benefits in terms of trust, rapport, and management far outweigh the cost in time. I once heard it said that the fourth "R," relationships, is the key to teaching the other three. Put differently, middle level kids often won't let you teach them until they know that you care about them.

An Idea: Teacher Journal. Strackbein and Tillman suggest that "you may want to write too, as a model" (1987, 29). For years, however, I had convinced myself that marginal comments and quick responses had met my students' needs for response. My thinking was changed by Sean.

I am writing all of this during play practice. Last contract it took me six entries to get this far. Journal writing is fun. If I keep this up you're going to have a lot of reading to do. There is one thing I mind—that is spilling my guts out to you and it's not that I don't trust you but I feel like your [sic] just someone I met in the street…

- Firm *but* flexible
- Client-centered (*like* kids)
- Supportive, *but* do not praise falsely
- Have a good sense of humor
- Can establish a climate that is humane and accepting *but* also task-oriented
- Advocates for kids (bend the bureaucracy)
- Remember what is was like!

Figure 3–1. Potpourri: Teacher qualities for middle level

Here he quickly changed the subject to something less threatening. I wrote a brief note in the margin to the effect that he was not required to "spill his guts" and that he could write about safer topics if he cared to—in essence, I put the ball back in his court. He continued the discussion in the next day's entry:

> That was definitely a very bad term to use. Did you ever write to someone you never knew. They seem like you know them like your best friend but then when you think about it you hardly know any thing about them. All I know is your name and some stuff I picked up from you talking to us. (Your name, your Parents are divorced and your mom remarried, you have a cat, you broke your arm, you drive a VW.) I am writing this because it is easier to do it this way I can explain it better.

I interpreted this as a suggestion that there be more balance in the disclosure by student and teacher. I wrote back that the time factor, not a reluctance to reveal myself, prevented me from sharing. Then it dawned on me that I could keep my own journal, which I started immediately. I used the same type of composition book, and the intended readers were all interested students in my classes. The book was kept (for public consumption) next to their turn-in station. I told the students that if they were interested (most were) they could read it at their leisure, as long as they returned it to the designated locale. The journal affords me the opportunity to reflect and reveal at opportune times.

Things That Kids Say. For students, keeping a journal can foster both personal growth and rapport with an adult. Additionally, the habit of free flow in writing down thoughts and reactions seems to stimulate thought processes that can later be channeled to writing the critical rough drafts of more formal papers. According to Fulwiler (1978), journalistic writing is at the heart of the writing process, involving conception, exploration, incubation, revision, and the eventual completed draft.

The alert teacher can learn a great deal diagnostically about students' writing skills, in addition to the students' thoughts. Each journal is a personal record of growth in language awareness. In nearly every case, fluency increases along with communication.

Victoria discusses several common middle school concerns, namely, the youngsters' emerging interest in the opposite sex, school pressure, and parental expectations—often as they relate to supposed comparisons with siblings. The simple act of thinking through such problems and putting them down on paper has a cathartic effect.

> I am in reading class right now—and I'm worried I won't finish my book in time. Today is the Thanksgiving dance. I'm getting really excited about it. It's fun to run around and ask boys to dance, and dance with boys, and dance with my friends. When the dance is over, my friends and I go to Burger King, and meet other

people. The only thing bad about the dances is you have to do all your home work at 7:30, and sometimes I have to stay up a long time to get it finished. But dances I think are the highlights of the school year. My mom always wants to know whoever I dance with. Sometimes that makes me mad!

It seemed like tonight the only place I could get any privacy and quiet to write my journal is in the bathroom! My sister is really bugging me tonight. All she ever talks about is Mike, and Don, and Josh, and Kyle! My mom says when I'm in 10th grade I'll be the same way. I'm back! I like writing in a journal. We just got it today. Maybe I should start a diary.

My parents always say that I have this terrific brain, but really I don't think they know that I'm not the brain they think I am. In our family I think that Joy is considered the beauty and I'm the brain, but really I don't think I'm either. What I'm trying to say is I think they expect more from me than Joy (grades wise).

In an era when young people feel that adults are unwilling to listen, journals aid in promoting the positive student attitudes that can have such an important impact on learning.

Collages: Connotations of Lyrics (Menu 11)

Kids love music and movies: Why not harness the trendiness of the age group? My students may negotiate to write the words of a favorite song or poem in the center of a piece of poster board, then create a collage that conveys the connotations and denotations of the lyrics. Students may choose to explain their choices and subtle thoughts to their peers. My students have created collages of everything from "God Bless America" to "Goodnight Saigon," from Five for Fighting to Janet Jackson. Again, teachers need to be vigilant regarding taste. These kids really scrutinize the pictures and the lyrics.

Other Writing/Poetic (Menus 12, 13, 14, 15, 16, and 17)

I'll share Meredith's poem:

Confusion
Who?
What?
Where?
When?
Why?
Questions,
they are so befuddling,
ringing in your mind,
like a resonant telephone,
just waiting to be answered.

The children may negotiate to do the usual formula poems (cinquains, diamente), but they really rise to the challenge of illustrating an emotion and describing it poetically. This enables them to explore and develop artistic talents as well.

Some children enjoy creating original short stories, writing author research, choosing their own adventures, and doing other research. The author research piece is usually thematic; Greg read several works by Sir Arthur Conan Doyle, for example, and chose to learn more about him. The written piece in this case was shared with the class and piqued further interest among his peers. Matt, on the other hand, negotiated to write and illustrate a compendium of reworked and enhanced fairy tales for his little sister.

Another popular genre for my kids is original plays. Two of my young ladies undertook the creation of a play called *Romeo and Julio* about gay, star-crossed lovers in New York City. They adapted a plot ingeniously (as *West Side Story* was adapted from Shakespeare, as Shakespeare adapted . . .). In my students' drama, Romeo was led to believe that Julio was dying from AIDS. Just as the quarantine prevented Shakespeare's Romeo from getting word in Mantua about Juliet's true condition, an accidentally erased voicemail never got to Romeo, and he took his own life. The girls negotiated to write a controversial piece, and their parents were kept informed. Also popular is the writing of children's books. Peter and Chad wrote a story for younger children called *Robbie Learns a Lesson*. With a clear and deliberate sense of the audience they created a charming little story with an antidrug message and read it to a third grade class.

Original Trivia Questions and Answers (Menu 20)

I find this activity to be terrific for developing true attention to punctuation and spelling. The children love this activity, which I use as a *sponge* throughout the year as I engage them in writing their own questions and answers to add to the deck of 3 × 5 inch cards. They have to think categorically. They have to write or type neatly and legibly. They must have a sense of audience. They also need substantive content—they must make a lot of cross-curricular connections to their science and social studies classes. Finally, they need to spell and punctuate in letter-perfect fashion, and they have a good time at the same time they are learning.

A Little More on Balance and Negotiation

Returning to the contract samples I shared earlier, it is important to connect the negotiable and nonnegotiable parts of the contract to those three big questions presented previously: Want to know? Need to know? Already know? Again note that the purpose of the first contract is to ease the students into responsibility and to enable them to do quality work and manage time and resources. Early contracts should be heavy on the nonnegotiable (i.e., required) side—kids still have choices concerning what book they read, possibly how they respond, and the like. They also exercise options as to when and where and in what sequence they do their tasks. Early on, I liken the challenge to undertaking a big meal: You may choose to eat all of your chicken before you start on your macaroni, or you can take a bite or two of one, then another, then back to one. You can map out a plan, or you can change in the middle as your tastes and whims dictate.

What is critical is for my students to assess themselves along the self-directed continuum (Tomlinson, see Figure 1–1, again), as well as for me to know where they are. Students who function well in a teacher-centered framework are not necessarily great contract workers. Similarly, some students who are pretty turned off by didactic instruction really thrive under contracting parameters. To muddy the waters more, a self-directed, ambitious learner might temporarily morph into his or her evil twin for a variety of reasons—social, family, hormonal. And those behaviors come and go. There is no typical middle level learner.

As the contracts gradually get longer and the options for negotiation widen, the menu (see Appendix, p. 102) is more and more important for both the teacher and the students. In the Appendix (p. 107) is an example of a largely negotiable contract that provides for a large degree of student autonomy that makes much use of the menu. To illustrate how it works in practice, here's a recreation of a negotiation session with Mike. It's the second day of contract number three scheduled for five weeks, mid April to late May. Yesterday, the class received the contract, a journal book, and a nonnegotiable crossword set, as well as their previously used guideline sheets and menus. They all know that they must build in a book choice and at least one major writing project. Last night they were to pencil in some preliminary choices. Mike has signed up to negotiate; he comes forward.

ME: How are you doing today, Michael? (Small talk, and so forth.)

MIKE: Fine. I know what I want to do. (He's not a small-talking kind of kid.)

ME: Okay. Let's have a look . . . . (Mike opens folder.)

MIKE: I definitely want to see *Platoon*. My dad said he'd rent it and watch it with me. It's rated R, but I can handle it okay. He was in 'Nam.

ME: Do you want to get the book version and do the compare and contrast project? Or do you want to do a separate movie summary and critique?

MIKE: I want to just do the summary and critique of the movie. I'll write it. And Ryan got a book about 'Nam called *In Country*. He says it's really good. I want to build that in.

ME: How about response? To *In Country*?

MIKE: Can I wait? Let me tell you what else I want to do. . . .

(Mike likes crossword puzzles, he definitely wants to do two extra sets. He is not crazy about lots of formal writing, but he's very interested in Vietnam and he agrees to write a short report on the war coupled with an interview with his father. We decide on length and parameters for his writings. There is still the issue of how to respond to *In Country*. He decides to build it into his journal. By this time we've decided on some things and have both written some items on the contract. He knows he can *flex* for extra credit as necessary, and that he can renegotiate if he chooses.)

ME: Okay, Mike. So in addition to crossword set 1, your five journal pages, and your formal Vietnam report plus interview you are going to. . . .

MIKE: See *Platoon* and write a movie summary and critique. And I'm gonna read *In Country* and I'll write a journal entry at the end of every chapter.

ME: And I'll respond to your entries. Be sure to use your "I Prompts" handout, and don't forget to predict a lot. Are you comfortable with the load? Okay. Have a parent sign off and keep me posted.

The negotiation with Mike is easy because he has a pretty good idea of what he wants to do. Negotiation requires some nudging without being onerous. It also requires being able to limit kids when they want to undertake too much. I've learned from experience that it is important to try to get the major products down and solidified—the kids can always come back for more of the smaller tasks for extra credit.

As I conclude this chapter, I reflect with pride on how my students respond to their rights and freedoms. They are proud, they work hard, and they collaborate effectively and efficiently. Each student has tasks at an appropriate level of difficulty, and I have high but achievable expectations of all students. The kids undertake work that they can complete only with some effort, so as to engender feelings of increasing competence and pride. I am at times rendered unnecessary, which at least occasionally should be a goal for all teachers. In subsequent chapters, more anecdotes, samples, and concrete examples are presented.

4

Handling the Load

*Fairness is doing what each child needs to be successful; it does
not mean doing the same thing for all children.*
—Don Holdaway

This chapter delves into handling the paper load, as well as the political and emotional exigencies of contracting. You will need, most likely, some support from key individuals in your organization. You'll also need to grow incrementally.

Differentiation of instruction is hard, hard work. For that matter, any good teaching is difficult and messy. I am here to admit to you that some learned people have looked at my writing on learning contracts and said "So what?" in that what I am describing is just plain good instruction, that one does not need a learning contract to have students produce the kind of work I describe in Chapters 2 and 3. But these individuals have not been afforded the joy and opportunity of seeing first hand the work that, say, Caroline and Brian chose to undertake. They did not spend 180 days with Gilberto, watching him, nurturing him, teaching him, learning with him—as he changed from angry young man to a producer of good work, proud of his growth in literacy.

Contracts allow the freedom and choice and responsibility for kids—and the freedom and time and purpose for teachers—to think about and create quality. Without the classroom culture fostered by contracting, Brian would never have had the incentive nor the time nor the intention of writing an eighty-page choose your own adventure that first borrowed Louis L'Amour's protagonist, Vincent Sackett, and then enhanced him in a manner that old Louis would certainly have approved of. I could never have handled the correction load, been the cheerleader, been the coach and enabler, and I absolutely could not have turned my back on the bulk of my students in order to give individual or small group attention for long chunks of time with absolute trust, had it not been for the contracting culture, the seriousness of purpose, and the structured choices.

For several years I have held on to copies of exemplars by Matt and Caroline, both of whom are presently pursuing graduate degrees in writing. The original products were beautifully illustrated in color and bound; the overall esthetic quality is diminished somewhat in the photocopying process, but the quality of writing by these twelve year olds is still apparent. It's clear that with choices and audience young adolescents put forth the extra effort that doesn't come with on-demand, prompted, structured assignments contrived by some ubiquitous unknown other.

As I mentioned earlier and is discussed more thoroughly in Chapter 8, individuals in the process of change are quick to revert back to what they always did when faced with opposition. The focus of this chapter is on helping you, no matter how far you are (or are not) on the continuum, to be proactive, and to incrementally handle the load. I elaborate on the tips for getting started from Chapter 2. Getting to the point where Jeff is, walking around and serving as a helpful consultant, dropping in and being able to focus on engaged and happy learners is a joy. I truly have many days when I feel guilty about being paid—I really am having that much fun. At any rate, in this chapter I flesh out the tips for getting started, but I also offer some practicalities for the structured choices allowed via learning contracts.

Remember: It's Easier to Get Forgiven Than to Get Permission

If the notion of a student-centered, differentiated classroom is new to you, you will of course want to start small. When you do start, you'll analyze your own zone of proximal development as well as your students' needs, wants, and thresholds. As you experiment with differentiated tasks and chunks of time, my best advice is that it's usually not necessary to inform your principal every step of the way. First of all, if you're the kind of teacher who's reading this book (you obviously are), then you're probably fairly well respected to begin with. Second, you may not know exactly where you're going and how things will look until you get there. So what is the need for too much hype and hoopla while you are learning? It's just added pressure—let the kids teach you a little, learn from you a little, and then do a demo lesson for your principal or other visitor. Which brings me to my next point. . . .

Know Thy Principal

The support of your building level instructional leader will be a key to your success. Remember the earlier "I'll come back when you're teaching" scenario? Be sure to assess your principal's readiness and invest in him or her in terms of capacity and understanding. Contracting is not expensive or faddish; don't launch into it with pleas for increased budgeting. Know when to flatter, when to spread credit around, and when to fall on your sword. Do whatever is necessary to *be a con artist for kids*. That is our ultimate goal—to help kids. We need to figure out the smoothest route for children—whether it be over, under, around, or through the building principal—but better in partnership.

Know Thyself

It is critical that you be willing to examine your philosophy of teaching and learning to meet individual needs. You need to project the potential payoffs for your students when weighed against the possible drawbacks. Stay within your zone early on, but be prepared to stretch. You're most likely not the type of teacher who wants to teach one year thirty times (how did I know that?), but at the same time you'll need to be ultrareflective as you grow in theory and in practice.

If you ask the right questions, you'll get compelling answers to stay the course. Big questions such as the following will make it hard to go back to being a skill-and-drill, multiple-choice type of teacher:

- Do learners care if they have choices about what and how to learn?
- Do some students process information in a different manner and at a different pace?
- Should you do most of the work in the classroom, or should students be the primary workers?

We really need to consider the macro issues, our personal essences about living and learning, before we focus on the activities, the stuff we do or have kids do. Practitioners are always eager for the practicalities and are at times impatient with too many whys—they want the hows. The hows in this book are necessarily intertwined with the whys. If you are with me for the most part on those three questions above, you are ready for the *must do* items that follow. Your individual paths may diverge somewhat, but you should find much of the following useful.

Start Small

In addition to starting small, a corollary is to give breaks from the intensity of contracting and not to spend too much time on a good thing. Remember that overfamiliarity can breed burnout. The kids need breaks, and you do as well. Be sure to consider the developmental appropriateness of the assignments that you require, as well as what the students choose. Teachers and students alike relate how they can become overly ambitious in their zeal to perform well during contract time.

Consider for a moment the words of sixth grader Kaitlyn D'Arcy, who was asked to give some thoughts on contract learning.

> Contracts are good because they give you lots of stuff to do like writing, presentations, and other kinds of projects. They always give you something to do and some of it is a lot of fun like making posters of animals and things like that. There is a lot of writing to do with the contracts too. Like stories we can make up, think it over comprehension questions, writing newspaper stories and even doing vocabulary questions. It's fun . . . but there is a catch, you always feel like you have something you could be doing that could be good but sometimes it isn't because sometimes you want to relax but you can't because you have the contract you could do.
>
> —*Kaitlyn D'Arcy*

Kids don't mind having lots of stuff to do. But notice what Kaitlyn says about "the catch." As teachers, you must develop a feel for when the students and you need to break from the rigors of contract learning.

Ease into contracting with small, deliberate, thoughtful, well-organized changes. If you're a true novice, your first contract may entail having all of your students complete an *anchor activity*, which is respectful work done individually and silently. You simply have the kids all work on a common piece of some sort. Over time this can grow to two activities, one for all and one an individual choice. Tomlinson (1999) espouses these activities and points out the paradox of

starting differentiation by not differentiating. She states quite cogently that you are paving the way for breaking off individuals or small groups to do other tasks while the bulk of the class has the independence to continue with a comfortable, predictable activity.

Teach and Model the Requisite Social and Management Skills

Speaking of paving the way, you must gradually move your classes toward success and independence without burdening them with too many changes and structures. As I mentioned earlier, there are many overlaps between my classes whether they are on or off contracts. The basic rules are the same, many of the routines are the same, and the trust is a constant—but it is when they are on contracts that things are put together so completely. The twelve-inch voices, the visual cues that cut out extraneous talk—these are practiced after being explained, demonstrated, and explicitly taught. My children hear me say, respectfully, that "Teaching isn't talking and learning isn't listening . . . it's just the opposite." At the same time, they are acutely aware of the culture of collaboration and that context and purpose are intrinsically related to the use of language.

Again, Kaufman's (2001) analysis of Linda Rief's management is very useful. Her philosophy regarding rules is based on being student centered. Typical *traditional* rules

serve to inhibit movement and sound in order to facilitate transmission-type teaching, whereas she seeks to promote students as active agents who require movement and sound. In fact, Kaufman uses the word *exploit* in the nonpejorative sense, in that Rief teaches her eighth graders to exploit movement, freedom, and her class structures.

I seek a middle ground, for I explicitly teach many procedures and I do have a few rules. Rules do not need to be adversarial. Middle level youngsters want some regulations; they do not do well with chaos and uncertainty. They do, quite reasonably, want some shared governance. And they are perfectly fine with rules that make sense to them—by extension, if they develop the classroom rules, it is just another example of their ownership and investment.

Set Goals, and Grow Slowly

Stick to the goals you set for yourself—but make sure that they are reasonable. Find the balance between the underestimation of your capabilities versus trying to do too much, too soon. Some possibilities for goals include, but are not limited to:

- Learn how to gauge how much work to allow kids to negotiate for, as well as how much work to require. This is a hard one, especially as you build to longer contracts.
- Resolve to take anecdotal notes on your students daily. (More suggestions will follow in the assessment/evaluation section.) This does not mean take notes on every child, every day, of course. Depth is far better than breadth. Make every effort to gain insights as to what works and what doesn't for each learner.
- Look carefully at student work. Expect and demand solid effort and care. Be sure to save exemplary work samples, as mentioned in Chapter 2. Challenge students to work toward exemplar quality.
- Assess students before, during, and after units, topics, whatever *stuff* they do. Remember that assessment is recursive and should constantly inform. Share rubrics, and do away with any type of *gotcha* mentality.
- Move toward more student choices. You still are final arbiter, but you'll get better, more careful work when they have leeway as to what they do, when they do it, and with whom.

Other Helpful Hints

Following are some other things to consider over time. These issues have come up repeatedly in my own experience, as well as for teachers I've mentored and interviewed.

Distribute the Students' Work Load (and Yours)

Your students will churn out a lot of excellent products that merit your response. As mentioned in Chapter 2, particularly if you are not in a self-contained situation, it is critical to (a) respond to their work as it is created and (b) assign the turn-in time (if you have multiple classes) so that all classes are not on contracts at the same time and whichever classes are on have different turn-in dates. Additionally, you may choose to stagger intra-class turn-in times—the work is already differentiated, so why not have them turn in the final products over an extended time, as opposed to on a single day?

As the adult in charge, you'll know who your procrastinators are. An occasional tweak or reminder that you need to see some products along the way is accepted and reasonable. Beverly Tihansky is a sixth grade teacher in a middle school who has been using learning contracts for over twenty years. On Mondays during contract time she has her sixth grade students map out on the board what they finished over the weekend and what their goals are for the week. This is a form of public positive peer pressure—she creates a grid that gives a visual, tangible representation of those who are falling a bit too far behind.

Assessment, Grading, and Reporting

Some of the most frequently asked questions I get about contracting relate to grading and assessment. In my mind, *assessment* is critical and informative, whereas grading is an institutional expectation that must be wrestled with and sometimes finessed.

Assessment literally means "to sit beside," and I see assessment as a partnership among my students and myself. Particularly during contracting times, my assessment is much more formative than summative—a sports analogy is that I am coaching in a scrimmage, teaching in the best sense as opposed to in a game. I offer my own help, plus feedback from parents and peers, to help make products exemplary. The ultimate goal is for my *workers* to internalize what constitutes quality and to strive for it. Due to the constant, purposeful feedback loop during contracting time, there are few surprises. Major pieces eventually are scored on rubrics, but a lot of what my kids do are simply *pass* items—there is no such thing as fail, there is only *fix* or *redo*.

To deal with the grading and evaluation conundrum, I do assign a total point value to most of my contracts. Because I am still bound to assign a letter grade for each student for each quarter, I find it easiest to extrapolate information to convert to grades that match the system. The classic questions that bedevil any reporting system are not totally resolved:

- How much does effort count?
- What about growth/improvement?
- What about homework?
- Class participation?
- Group work?

In direct contrast to all of the previously mentioned items, which many teachers do use to factor a grade, is the bottom-line question:

- Achievement against the standard?

I tend to be idiosyncratic and client-centered in my grading, while keeping the standards in mind. Whereas some teachers use grading as a cudgel, in my contracting system it is more like a carrot—and at payoff, icing on the cake.

I want my students to see assessment as clear, frequent, and constructive feedback, so that they are able to see growth in their capacities and skills. My bottom line with most of these youngsters is *quality rules*. I want children to self-assess and do their best. Let's face it, they're typically not accumulating grade point averages that officially *count* in middle schools. I structure my grading to be user friendly, generous, and collegial.

Stay Organized

I tend to be somewhat random in my organization and am also a bit of a pack rat. As a saver, I am faced at times with *retrieval* problems. Orchestrating contracts really forces me to be better organized. I must carefully think through and explicitly communicate my room arrangement (see Figure 2–1, page 13) and my expectations, protocols, and routines.

I also shared the organization load with my students. They have access to both their dump (i.e., storage) portfolios and their working contract portfolios. I put them in charge of storage and retrieval—my aforementioned problem area. I take responsibility for some of the requisite storage and retrieval, but they ease the load by exercising their free access to the dump portfolio, alphabetizing, and moving materials from *active* to *retired* status (and recursively back again) as the context warrants.

Establish Procedures for Routines

One of the biggest positive aspects of contracting is the enhanced control of time. Students need to be explicitly taught how to maximize this most precious commodity. I've seen teachers use egg timers with bells very effectively when contracting, but I never chose to—it was too Pavlovian. Beverly Tihansky is adamant about not wanting to waste any class time. Whereas I have my seventh graders sign up on the board for conferences/teacher consultation, she has devised a *pick a number* management tool, just like at the delicatessen. As students enter the room, they go to a designated box and take a large, laminated number, go to their seats or work stations, and then go to her for turn-in, or conference, or feedback in sequence, according to their chosen numbers.

You'll want to think about your start-up and wrap-up procedures. Early in the year, I expect students in their home base seats, at work, quiet. There may be a little bit of traffic to their dump portfolios or to the designated sign-up area for conferences, but I will not talk to them or entertain any questions until they are all on task. Then I either go around individually to answer questions, modeling twelve-inch talk all the way ("May Tara and I work on our children's book?" "May Gabe and I do puzzle set one together?") or do it from the front of the room. Once pairs are situated, I'll make brief announcements if necessary, set up any flex groups for minilessons, and let them settle in. After the working time, I typically give a three-minute warning, bring them all back to their home base seats, and possibly engage in a quick whole class activity, crossword puzzle seminar, book talk or update, or some type of closure.

New teachers are understandably apprehensive about classroom management and promoting movement and peer collaboration seems illogical to those who want to be "sage on the stage." Kaufman (2001) talks about how Linda Rief focuses a great deal of time teaching procedures: "However, to the novice language arts teacher as well as to skeptics, the two months Linda spent addressing organizational and management issues to the point of student internalization may seem extraordinary, perhaps even inordinate" (122).

My analogy has always been akin to the old road construction signs: "Temporary inconvenience, permanent improvement." Although I do not devote the amount of "procedural preteaching" time that Linda Rief does, she and I agree that the focus on procedures should not be at the expense of quality literacy instruction—rather it is necessary for the students to exploit new freedoms of choice and time.

Don't Feel Compelled to Grade Everything

Remember that students can self-correct many things created under contract—this is to their advantage as well as yours. Additionally, peer correction is a viable alternative. I have even involved parents in grading—that was a bit of a risk, but it paid off. I had involved parents for years as proofers of student work, asking that they sign off after, for example, doing anything from a content conference to an editing job.

Kids, of course, enjoy peer response—but, as always, you'll need to be vigilant. Beverly Tihansky is adamant about the near-impossibility of her even attempting to respond to all student work herself. She is particular as to what she *grades*, leaving much of the response load to designated others.

Don't Fret About Standards (Too Much)

In the present political and academic environments we are certainly cognizant of the standards movement. *Accountability* is trumpeted—and with standards come evaluation. In most districts, teachers feel great pressure to see to it that students attain or exceed the standards. Standards have been proffered as reasonable targets for all to attain, to ensure that all students learn what matters. Unfortunately, when teachers are pressured (internally, externally, overtly, covertly) to *cover* standards in order to get students ready for the high-stakes tests, genuine learning is often hobbled. James Popham (2001), for example, has written compellingly and authoritatively about uses and misuses of standardized tests.

Curriculum differentiation needs to be the partner of standards-based initiatives, for *standards* and *standardization* do not mean the same thing. According to Debra Burns (2002), teachers must preassess and differentiate. "When someone says, 'I know my kids; I don't need to preassess,' what that really means is, 'I know what the average kid in my room is capable of, and that's what I'm teaching to"(3). Yet Burns maintains, and rightfully so, that we'll get what we always got if we continue to teach to the middle. She says that what is necessary is to have a decent baseline and a high ceiling. Although she is not talking about contracting per se, she could be—the underpinnings are essentially the same.

Teachers and students absolutely need to examine and work with the standards lists. In the late 1990s, I assembled a team of about thirty-five teachers of literacy to rewrite the district's language arts curriculum in alignment with the new draft of the proposed standards for our state. We worked for three long hard days that summer and had a running joke about the inclusion of the *virgule* at standard 1.5.11 F related to the quality of writing. At that time, I had earned a doctorate and a wide array of experiences in the language arts, and I had never heard of the word. It turned out that I knew what it was and (more importantly) how to use it, but the committee still had a jocular time, conjecturing as to how the state was going to assess proficiency in the use of virgules. I work with teachers who are adamant that our state's literacy standards are best taught through a variety of authentic, meaningful contexts. Contract learning allows the students to apply the important skills and strategies in meaningful ways. Contracting provides them the time, opportunity, and flexibility to meet individual needs, reteach explicitly when necessary, and provide interesting, challenging opportunities for a variety of students.

They find that teaching skills in isolation is hollow, inane, abstract, and difficult for teachers and children. Regarding the entire *coverage* enterprise, it's like the salesman who claimed he sold it, but that the client didn't buy it. We are foolish to teach mechanics without meaning; it flies in the face of what we know about human learning.

Contracting allows for coherent learning. Under contracts, teachers can effectively teach to the standards, at times *pulling out* the necessary pieces, but always putting them back into context.

Recently, for example, I needed to address the standard for using dialogue in narrative writing. In the classes on contract at the time, I did the direct instruction with the whole class in the form of a fifteen-minute minilesson, using three samples of kids' works on the overhead projector. I then pulled aside eight of the students to work on a couple of exercises out of context in an effort to be systematic; I then had them apply the targeted conventions as they returned to their authentic narrative writing.

Don't Fret (Either) Testing

You don't fatten your sheep by weighing them more. Kids will read and write better when they read and write a lot. Teach them to think, to self-monitor. Provide them time to practice. Give them targeted instruction in strategies. The scores will take care of themselves. Aimee Buckner (2002) offers her belief that "If you teach well, maintain best practices, make instructional decisions based on your students' needs, and make decisions that are reflective of your pedagogy; your students *will* learn. They will learn well, and they will pass the test" (215). She also offers a top ten list for maintaining excellence in teaching in an environment of testing.

Yes, high stakes tests have become a reality in the lives of teachers and students. We cannot afford to ignore these tests, since the results may be (and are) used to make life-altering decisions about children, programs, and teachers. But helping kids learn to read does *not* begin with the test.

Contracting means the opportunity for children to read a lot, and wide reading results in better reading (Tierney and Readence 2000). Fielding and Pearson (1994) also remind us that sufficient time for actual text reading is paramount to ensure improved reading. They cite research that is unequivocal regarding the evidence that both able and struggling readers benefit from engaged reading time, as opposed to isolated skills instruction. Additionally, structures that allow targeted instruction that is based on the student's needs make sense for all learners.

Yes, there will be a load to handle. Yes, there will be risks to take. But the rewards will far outweigh the drawbacks. Stay the course! Your kids will not disappoint you.

5

Yeah, But...

The hollowness of the informational approach may be seen in the fact that far too many youngsters in this country can name the parts of speech but can't put them together to say what they mean, can tell you what onomatopoeia is but hate poetry.

—JAMES MOFFETT

A naysayer can find plenty of reasons not to do contracts. When kids are trusted and empowered and explore topics of interest, certain problems can and do arise. Following are an array of the thorny issues that I have been able to address, usually with success, over the years.

More on Censorship and Taste Issues

When children are free to make choices, teachers need to be aware of family and community mores. I give middle schoolers pretty free rein and find that it is best to be proactive. Regarding assigned texts, I have a responsibility to not offend any child with my choice. With self-selected texts, however, my responsibility (and ours as a learning community) is to respect and understand the tastes of others; it also is incumbent on me to make it clear that the imprimatur of the school is not to be assumed just because a book is read as part of school credit.

To do this, I start off each year with a letter to parents, which I discussed earlier (see Appendix, p. 106). The essence is that it is critical to engage kids with print, but that I cannot monitor every choice carefully. If the choice was copacetic at home, I would honor parental judgment. One of my ninth graders some years ago was very motivated by *Hammer of the Gods*, which chronicled the deeds and misdeeds of Led Zeppelin. It was pretty graphic and lewd and bawdy—but then, so were the *Canterbury Tales*. The young man read thoughtfully and responded, per his contract, appropriately. For his next choice we agreed on a *shopping list* book by H. G. Welles.

I am candid with middle schoolers about *ratings* of books—we have developed a sort of rubric for books and adapted the MPAA rating system. I want my kids to be sensitive to specific criteria as opposed to a single criterion. We talk about Roald Dahl's bad taste (to some), as well as controversial and colorful authors such as Oscar Wilde and Truman Capote. Some of my present students have negotiated to undertake projects dealing with the most censored schoolbooks. We also wrestle with rating and taste issues in movies. When they do the compare and contrast project discussed earlier, they are at times required to discuss the MPAA rating and why it is merited (or not).

Confidentiality (Particularly in Journals)

As with book selection, I am open about my promise that what they write will be strictly confidential unless it involves something illegal or someone getting hurt. I delved into this matter in some detail earlier in Chapter 3. Several years ago, a young man was quite depressed and wrote in his journal about wanting to hurt himself. I wrote back that I wanted him to go the guidance office immediately. He did. Otherwise, I would have breached confidentiality. A proactive response is needed in that type of situation.

At times children have told me more than I really wanted to know about home situations—they would not have had the opportunity to express this orally, but some have written some rather startling things. What they wrote was at times poignant, at times bittersweet, and often not for the faint of heart. Angie wrote, for example, about an encounter or skirmish that was somewhat amusing and that also shared a lot of insight. Her parents would probably have been chagrined had they known that she wrote this. I did not encourage this type of revelation, and I had to be careful how I responded.

Hi Dr. G! I'm writing this from my room, I'm grounded again. At least until my dad gets home. Here's what happened.

I'm REALLY tired of my mom treating me like a servant. I don't mind doing chores around the house, I live here too and I can help, but I HATE it when she orders me around. That's how I got grounded.

See I got home today after school, and Chris (my little brother) and I were in the kitchen, and my mom ordered me to go down to the basement refrigerator to get her a soda. She does that all the time. I was really mad, but I didn't talk back, I went down and got a can of Pepsi and I shook it *really* hard all the way upstairs.

Then I innocently handed it to her and stood way back. Of course it sprayed all over the place, when she opened it. It was sticky all over the counter and the walls. She knew it immediately and yelled and sent me to my room. I said under my breath, "Good, it was worth it." She didn't hear me, but my bratty brother heard me and tattled, and she said I was grounded for 3 weeks!

So here I am in my room, getting some work done on my contract. When dad gets home she'll tell him what happened and he'll un-ground me after they argue about it a while. It may even take a day or two, but it won't be any longer. They'll say it's because they love me.

Work Load (for Teachers)

As alluded to earlier, kids churn out a lot of work under the terms of contracts. I have had many observers in my classes other neighboring school districts; one commented: "That's way too much work." The key thing for me is to stagger the contracts two ways. As mentioned previously, only have two of the classes on contracts at a time, and I have those two due dates at least a few days apart. Another management aid involves resisting the need to respond personally to everything the children produce.

The other big help is to have the in/out boxes in use. It helps the kids to distribute their work and me to distribute mine. I am able to get to the important work of responding incrementally due to the fact that students handle much of their own loads by self-correcting. I am particularly careful to give good narrative feedback to their journals.

I can only say that the time I spend responding and giving feedback is worth it to me. All of the time and effort comes back to me many times over in effort, good cheer, good behavior, and pride in their work. Many other teachers that I've introduced to contracting have been just as pleased. Following are some excerpts from a letter sent to me by a contracting *convert* who I worked with in recent years. At the time he wrote the following, he was teaching sixth grade in a self-contained setting in a K–6 elementary school.

Here, in no particular order, are some things I love about contracts:

No wasted time! Hillary, one of those beautiful, perfect girls from DEEP (the district's gifted and talented program, notation mine) used to read an extra novel every week just by pulling out the book every time she had to wait for me. While I was getting all the rambunctious boys to sit down and taking care of the kids who hadn't remembered their pencils, or dealing with legitimate stuff like getting kids off to their instrumental lessons or scheduled medicines or appointments with Chapter One and resource room teachers . . . through all this time Hillary would be knocking out another Newbery novel. But those days of wasted time are over.

Now, after the first five minutes of Monday morning Hillary's got her work cut out for her. Hillary could never really get into something because she had to squeeze her freedom time out of those lost moments scattered throughout the school day. Pulling out a novel and reading a few pages was the best she could do with that chopped up time. Now, though, she can plow through the week's work in two or three days, and then get on with writing her play or building her robot.

And this new approach to wasted time drives the recalcitrant kids crazy. I had one boy in class who'd been clinically, scientifically, psychiatrically labeled "oppositional defiant.". . . When you've got a kid in class who's as smart as you are, but who's looking to vent his anger at his absent father by undermining everything you do in class, it's just very difficult to proceed in the old way. It's unbelievable how powerful a kid like that can be in slowing down a "lesson" when he starts with "can I borrow a pencil?" . . . "I forgot my book—can I go back to my room to get it?". . . "Hey look everybody, it's snowing" . . . "but do animals masturbate? Do fish?" Everything comes to a grinding halt. Most of the kids are as bugged by it as the teacher, because they just want to get on with it. . . .

With the contracts, there's no audience. Really, there's no stage. Instead of teacher on stage, with oppositional-defiant or class clown trying to get on and bump the teacher off, there's just every kid busy on his own . . . on his own stage I suppose. The malingerers are left to face their work. . . . Avoiding work is a way to avoid failure for many of them. It's more fun to be funny than to struggle through schoolwork that just rubs their noses in their real or imagined inadequacies in reading or writing. And right after one of these moments when another kid tells him off is a great time for me to stop by his desk and say, "You know Dave, you've got a lot of strengths you could build on. Let's work together a while to get you some momentum, and then let's see what you can really do when you put your mind to it."

We make better use of teacher time. I really have made that transition from "sage on the stage to guide on the side" that everyone's talking about. . . . (There is, however, an increase in requests for me to listen to a piece they've just written or an idea they've just hatched.) So I stroll around pretending I'm a consultant, suggesting resources, writing up library passes, looking over the kids' shoulders, encouraging, making time management suggestions, cracking a few jokes, smiling, playing. . . . It's as if they believe it's been handed down by the Department of Education or Congress or something, and I'm just this helpful guy who can join in and help them scale that mountain. And they see the contract, with the whole week's work assembled in one place in checklist form, as a kind of challenge. They take it personally in a way that they don't when the assignments come in small pieces in narrowly defined times and tasks. Maybe they feel more in control when they can see it all at once, without having to be dependent on the teacher to dispense it in small doses.

Kids are getting more responsible. Those complicated assignment book systems that are supposed to teach responsibility do just the opposite, I think. If you're getting your assignment book signed every day at school, and every night at home, and getting candy every time you do something right, with adults breathing down your neck all the time, you're just a trained seal. I think some of those kids at Penn State go berserk and drink all that beer because they've never really been free to develop responsibility. Contracts lead kids gradually through a process of developing the capacity to cope with freedom. And time management is something no daily assignment book can teach. . . . And I love to see kids learning from the natural consequences of their actions—enjoying the ease of a lazy Friday after hammering away all week, or enduring a Thursday night all-nighter that's been earned by slacking off too early. Even the insides of kids' desks are looking better. When they figure out that they've got to save the stuff they did Monday to turn in on Friday, or learn the hard way by doing the same thing twice because it fell out of the desk into the path of a conscientious custodian, they start remembering where they put things. They're more dependent on the contract document than on the teacher's constant directing, and it gives them a new respect for paper. Kids are more aware about grades, too. It used to amuse me that kids were always so shocked at report card time. It was like the academy awards, with obvious "A" students accepting their awards with humble and grateful surprise, and the kids who never did a lick of work all semester expressing disbelief, bewilderment, or moral outrage over a "C-" (or worse). They seemed to view the whole grading game as magic, and completely separate from anything they'd done or not done. But the contracts put the teacher's grade book in the kids' hands. They keep track the way they'd track their batting averages or bowling scores, and begin to accept responsibility for the outcomes of their work. By the way—I don't feel guilty about grading kids' papers in class anymore. I like to have kids sit with me while I'm looking over their work. I think out loud about the work as I'm evaluating it. It's more complete feedback than a letter grade and a quick written comment can provide.

Parent communication is built in. You've seen my revisions of my contracts. Now I have parents sign the day the new contract is first issued to the kids, and again when it's returned with a grade. I even have the work broken down into daily doses (the "recommended study plan") for those kids who need that kind of planning help in the early stages, and parents can use that like a daily assignment book if they like. Parents can never complain that they "weren't informed" about their kids' assignments or progress or performance. I don't have to call home to say which assignments weren't turned in or to ask why a failed quiz hadn't been returned with a signature. There's much less chasing around in this way because it's all in writing, all the time. For parents who aren't looking for a way to blame the teacher instead of their kids, but who just like to know where their tax dollars are going, it's all there for them, too. I think we have to get back to thinking of parents as partners in their children's education. The contract makes it easy for parents to see the whole picture of what I'm trying to do with their kids. . . .

The fun of educational design is a thing the contracts bring out into the open. Kids started making mature, sophisticated suggestions about what might be added or eliminated from contacts. They'd never get so deeply involved in helping teachers with their lesson plans, other than just to complain. It's a little like putting

Congress on cable TV. You just get more into it when you can see what's going on on the inside. I find that I enjoy the planning more. There's a continuous improvement energy that gets rolling when I return to last week's contract on my computer and start playing around with it to make it better for the next time.

As should be apparent from the above excerpt, the teacher was repeatedly assigning week-long contracts in a self-contained setting. Despite my cautions, he was so pleased with the results that he started burning his kids out. He eventually backed off. Please remember that kids need challenge, but they also need variety.

Work Load (for Kids)

My purpose is for kids to apply their evolving literacy skills and to enjoy themselves at the same time. Much of the pleasure of contracting stems from the aforementioned social aspects of learning and the natural desire to share quality work publicly.

I find it very important to be conscious of rates at which young learners produce. The same assignment takes some children considerably longer than it takes others. Students report that they work harder under contracts, but that it is more pleasurable. I find it easier to take things off their proposed plates—they could always be put back on as time permits. And remember, they are only on about one third of the year. As you gradually build from less negotiable projects and assignments to more open-ended/generative ones, you will gradually develop a sense of how much to stretch kids, as well as when to limit their zeal.

Dishonesty

Vignette: My second school district, again ninth grade English. I'm young and strong and without children of my own—but I'm teaching six English classes a day and two of the sections contain nearly forty kids. It is the Tuesday after Memorial Day weekend, and the last two sets of contracts are due at the end of the period. This class has thirty-eight kids, but I've staggered everything else, so I can get to the last contracts in time to factor in everything before exams. Rod comes to me, disconsolate, and nearly in tears. He explains to me that he took his contract with him to his parents' boat on the Chesapeake, to finish things up over the long weekend prior to turn-in. But he left the entire contract on the boat, three hours away. His father (a prominent local attorney) is poised to close down the office and drive the six-hour round trip to retrieve the folder containing all the work. I have never budged on contract deadlines in the past, and I have deadlines to meet due to the school calendar. But Rod is practically in tears, and I think of the six-hour drive for his father. I relent, telling him I'll take the contract the following Monday, nearly one week late, since his family goes back to the boat that weekend anyhow. Rod practically falls to his knees in gratitude.

Three years later, Rod is about to graduate. Another senior, Mark, tells me that Rod scammed on that contract; he had been procrastinating and told a tall tale in order to buy more time to finish his work. He even told several of his buddies about his deception. They must have been good friends, for none squealed. I just laughed. What else could I do?

Other than the Rod deception, I occasionally find a situation in which students copy or exchange work, but that is rare. Such transgressions usually occur due to poor time and workload management. My students are generally good about time and task management, but they do occasionally run into problems. Those who are poor managers often have to rush at the end of the prescribed time, resulting in less than best quality work and a lower than optimal grade.

Peer Relationships

Real-life human dramas sometimes unfold when students are bound by contract to collaborate. For example, Amanda and Tanya negotiated to undertake the creation of a rather ambitious short story. Coauthoring can be like a good marriage when everything works out, but problems can also arise. Amanda and Tanya planned and distributed the workload for their masterpiece carefully, and early in their project they were right on schedule in meeting with me to get feedback. Amanda was an ambitious, driven young lady, whereas Tanya was a bit more ethereal. As the deadline grew near, Tanya had an absence or two and failed to produce her expected contributions to the project. Amanda, impatient and frustrated, took over the work, changed things to her satisfaction, and turned in a solid piece by agreed upon due dates. She signed both names, but the work was almost entirely hers. Tanya was furious! She felt slighted and embarrassed—and felt no guilt or compassion for Amanda's plight. Of course, I needed to intervene. A three-way conference resulted in tears and recriminations. Only after a cooling-off period and some reflective writing were the girls able to forgive and understand each other.

Disorganization

This happens to adults as well, but contracting certainly requires and demands good organization on the part of students.

I stop short of explicit flexible groups for the organizationally challenged, but I am well aware of students who need more vigilant monitoring on my part. The incremental turn-in system with the in/out boxes really helps. In general, organizational issues are headed off with proactive reminders. Occasionally, important products are temporarily *lost*, and some anxious moments ensue, but things get safely turned in on time.

Professional Dissonance and Jealousies

This has never been an explicit issue in my experience, but it has the potential to be a divisive factor. Colleagues may see contracting as too child centered, too much fun, too soft. They also may feel that there is too much listening to children. Matt wrote in his journal:

> I am really having trouble with Mrs. Jones. I don't know why she went into teaching. She loathes children.

To the best of my knowledge the math teacher on my team never saw that entry, but problems could have erupted had I in any way divulged Matt's sentiments.

Just as my principal had looked askance at contracting at first, so did some of my teammates. Early in my middle school tenure I experimented with brief pilot contracts in partnership with the social studies and science teachers—we developed interdisciplinary contracts connecting our subjects, but my teammates were concerned about content coverage issues and things gradually fizzled. I did facilitate, however, some excellent interdisciplinary contract work in self-contained settings. Contracting is idiosyncratic enough that certain teacher characteristics are required to enable the magic to occur. Again, the work of Pitton (2001) is instructive, as she notes the need for constant reflection and self-examination. Gallagher-Polite (2001) followed the downward spiral of a retired-on-the-job veteran teacher: "She has given up on her desire to make a difference in the lives of her students and has been an observer and participant in her own demise" (27).

Parental Overinvolvement

This has been an occasional, tacit problem. Most of my contracts eventually require parent signoffs and approval. Most major written assignments require drafts and process samples to be attached, and the final product needs peer and adult proofers to sign. I occasionally suspect a bit of overinvolvement on the part of anxious or competitive parents, for the temptations and the opportunities are greater due to the loosening of teacher control of multiple tasks. My overall view, however, is that overinvolvement beats the heck out of underinvolvement.

Over many years, with thousands of students, the efforts and achievements have been satisfying and the problems have been few. Be proactive, but remember that you can't anticipate every potential problem. When the sense of community has evolved, kids as well as their parents are amazingly tolerant, resilient, and forgiving.

Monitoring Individual Progress

With certain students, under certain circumstances, I require the use of a *daily log* as part of the contract. Some years ago, I had all of my students do one, but for most of them it was not necessary; only the organizationally challenged were in need.

I found that my mental notes were usually good enough, but the human memory is faulty. The log makes the students responsible, and I can then spot check at critical junctures when I have questions. With all of the choices and options, the logs do, in fact, ease the pressures on me.

It looks like this:

Contract #2   **Name** _____

Log of Activities

Overall goals	_____
Monday 12/04	_____
Tuesday 12/05	_____
Wednesday 12/06	_____
Thursday 12/07	_____
Friday 12/08	_____
Goals for next week	_____
Comments	_____

I make it clear to my kids that they need to plan, but that it's acceptable to change plans as necessary. It's a combination log that allows them to plan what they expect to do, but they are permitted to record what was done retroactively.

Monitoring the Group: Those with Whom You're Not Engaged

Under contracts (as with, for example, guided reading) the power of instruction and engagement that takes place away from the teacher must rival the power that takes place with the teacher.

The biggest advantage of contracting is that it allows me to focus full attention on an individual or a small group (for guided reading, for example), without needing to manage the bulk of the class. Contracting is, in fact, *workshopping* time, but other routines and structure are easily layered on. It's analogic (at times during the day) to having centers going on at the same time the teacher runs guided reading groups. But under contract learning, *my* group might not meet daily and I might not instruct a kid for several days—and the center-like activities for the masses are much more student-controlled and fluid.

As with any good teaching, decisions under contracts need to be grounded in the teacher's knowledge of the children's developing literacy. As mentioned earlier, I teach my middle schoolers how to be independent. I want them to be engaged in appropriate activities—to be set up for success. They need to be able to choose from among a variety of activities that they'll value and be proud to share. My goal is to constantly monitor the abilities and the independence of the children. At the same time I must be sensitive to the external demands of the curriculum (and the accompanying standards and tests). Children must see contracting time as precious, accessible, and as purposeful.

Potential Downsides: Cautions

One of the young teachers I work with reviewed this book while it was being written. She is happy with the contracting culture that she has developed with her sixth graders, but she says that it was "expensive" in terms of energy spent and time lost. She said, in essence, that every article or book she reads that promotes an innovation "sounds so good" but often is not cautionary enough. She urged that I add a brief section that enumerates the possible dangers and pitfalls of contracting. Here, in no particular order, are things to watch out for.

Starting Slowly

This has been mentioned repeatedly. Take your time, and layer things incrementally. Try out short contracts and don't overwhelm yourself or your students. Plan carefully, but be prepared to be flexible.

Amount of Work Assigned

If you start slowly and build incrementally, you should avoid overchallenging or underchallenging your students. As your comfort level evolves, you shouldn't be afraid to renegotiate as circumstances warrant.

Quality of Work Assigned

Busy work is still busy work, even if part of a contract. Packets and subskill work should be targeted and should be put back into a meaningful context. Remember that all kids, particularly in the middle, need variety.

Faking It: Self-Management Issues

Mike was one of my challenges a few years ago. He was very high in energy and very short in attention span on a normal day, and the year that I was his seventh grade teacher his parents were going through an acrimonious divorce. He would *drift* constantly during direct instruction times, and homework was often a problem, largely due to a lack of consistency at home.

During the first contracts that year, Mike really floundered. He had a particularly difficult time with his independent reading. I'd watch him go to a space in the room, settle in, and pretend to read. Then he'd move to another spot and try for a while. Then he'd try to randomly tackle something else on the contract—usually without success. As I reflected on it, I knew I needed to be more directive. I also needed to let Mike struggle a bit. Due to the fact that the other children were fully occupied, I was able to really watch Mike and, when the time came, then devote undivided attention to him—which I did face to face in quiet conferences and via his journal.

The first problem was in his choice of individualized reading book. Despite his *on level* reading history on a variety of measures of comprehension, I assumed (wrongly) that the motivation factor would carry him through his choices, as had happened with many of my kids before. I moved from my usual nudging, cajoling mode to a gently directive one—after talking about his interests, I chose four books from which he could choose. We then mapped out a schedule for his reading, dividing the book for regular conferences.

We then, together, mapped out the three-week load for the entire contract much the same way. All of the kids conferred with me anyway, he just conferred more frequently, and with more care on my part. There also was much more *progress monitoring* dialogue in his journal. He grew to enjoy the attention, as long as it was unobtrusive. He eventually handled the workload and felt successful, as an autonomous learner.

Yes, the *yeah, but* attitude is out there. Be patient and be reflective.

6

Magic in the Middle

Writing is easy. All you have to do is sitdown at a typewriter and open a vein.
—RED SMITH

Differentiation of instruction is a hot topic, and contracts have been overlooked of late, but they are an important missing link in providing the individual attention that children deserve and require. When I ran this idea by several experts in the field, they were afraid that contracting would be seen as too passé in the present climate of high-stakes testing and standards. I believe, strongly, that precisely due to standards-based curricula and accountability, now more than ever, we must hear students' voices and enfranchise their learning.

Listen to some middle school teachers who are here and now doing their own versions of magic in the middle—trusting kids, facilitating their learning, and making good things happen.

Biff

Biff teaches language arts and mathematics to sixth graders in a nearby middle school. He was an economics major in college; he took an extra year to change to an elementary education major. He's now in his early thirties, growing professionally, using contracts to differentiate, motivate, and manage.

He teaches as part of a four-teacher team (language arts, science, social studies, and mathematics) of core teachers. He teaches two double blocks of language arts and a single period of math—he also has team planning and a personal preparatory period daily, in addition to advising. His team pioneered student-led parent conferences a few years ago, and he has spread the contracting word among teammates.

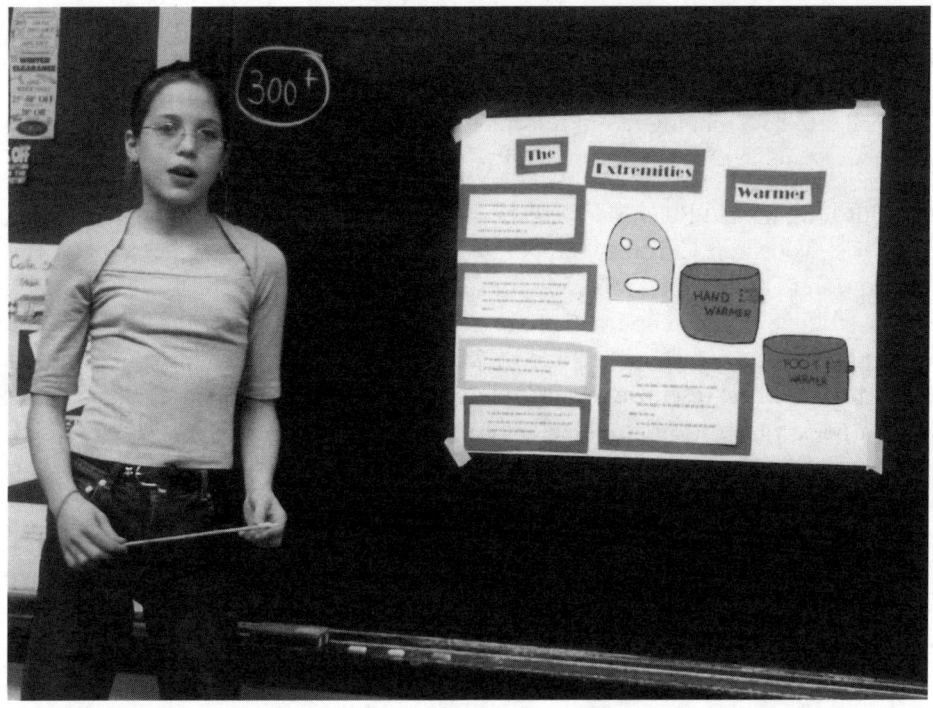

Biff shared with me his use of contracting in a survival unit. The springboard was reading aloud *The Girl Who Owned a City* by O. T. Nelson (followed by whole group roundtable discussions). The contract per se then started with student choices from among an array of *survival* staples (*Island of the Blue Dolphins, My Side of the Mountain, The Other Side of the Mountain, Call It Courage, The Hay Meadow, The River, Hatchet, Julie of the Wolves, The Sign of the Beaver*). The students selected their books (Biff and his student teacher, Miss Gray, did book talks on each title), read them independently or "paired"; special needs children had books on tape. The students then completed nonnegotiable activities and negotiable choices as stipulated in the contract and attachments (see Appendix, pp. 108 and 109).

Biff also has found contracting to be a powerful tool for managing many of his existing best practices. The research is clear (Anderson et al. 1985) about the impact of wide self-selected reading on reading comprehension scores. All good teachers know the value of independent reading and shared reading, and contracts really enhance the independent reading component. Biff put it this way:

The district sent me to a conference a few years ago, and I heard Lucy Calkins speak. She talked about the early days of SSR, how there was novelty in the teacher (and the custodian, and the cafeteria ladies) modeling for the kids. But Calkins said, and I remember well, that both the teacher and the kids were not accountable enough, that we needed to ratchet it up. I remember those kids that I was sure were faking it—but they faked it quietly. Calkins said that SSR time is better used for the teacher to do a running record or conference with a kid. I agree. Now, with contracts, I can have instant accountability.

Biff took his old Reader's Workshop model and layered his contract on. (See Reader's Workshop Contract, Appendix, p. 111). He says that he resisted the temptation to build in too much response, and that the process log was very quick and useful. He would keep track of previous menu choices to ensure variety—the students are responsible for keeping their menus safe and accessible. Biff said that sometimes the best response to a great book is no response, other than a quick talk with a peer, a parent, or the teacher. As you examine the Language Arts Menu (see Appendix, p. 102), you'll note that it's brief and uncluttered. Obviously, over time, Biff was able to talk about and model each of these and more. The fact that he had double blocks of time daily really helped. He was particularly fond of the *rehearsed reading* idea at the culmination of a self-selected reading. He would have the children *go public* with a dramatic or very interesting passage—this would pique peer interest, as well as building fluency, self-confidence, and reflection. Students were instructed to rehearse their chosen passage as much as they liked, and to put it in context it so that it made sense to their chosen audience. I was in this classroom recently and heard a young lady read a moving excerpt from *To Kill a Mockingbird*.

Teachers are rightfully concerned about content coverage issues. Biff has obligations to address certain skills and strategies and genres as laid out in the district curriculum, which are, of course, articulated with the state standards. In looking at the Partner Contract for Science Fiction/Fantasy (see Appendix, p. 113) you see what Biff termed a *partner contract* that harnessed positive peer interdependence, had the students engaged in sound instructional practices, and also covered the anthology selections that were called for.

Biff was very clear about eschewing black line masters and workbook pages—he believes they do not belong in contract packets. He does build in targeted skill masters for specific needs—that is, if a child needs practice on strong action verbs, in addition to working on the need in context, he'll pull out the need and assign the skill sheet. He said that occasionally his students enjoy the almost immediate gratification of a quick activity that is done as opposed to process-oriented and ongoing work.

The final contract set from Biff is related to a specific text: *Sounder*. For *Sounder*, see the example of a Group Interdependence type of contract (see Appendix, p. 114 and Figures 6–1 and 6–2). Note the customized rubric and the

management grid. Biff's rubrics are stored on his computer and are easily adapted. In the set Biff provided, all students were assigned the book, but there is choice and negotiation built in, as well as the student-friendly use of clear evaluative criteria.

Doug

Doug is one of my protegees who teaches seventh grade language arts. He has high energy and is innovative. He needed to be reined in a bit when he first started with contracts. He was very pleased with the quality of his students' work and was also very happy with parental feedback. The kids were happy with the newness of

Team Name_____ Name_____ Novel_____

Week	Teammates	Vocabulary Precision	Catchall	Characterization	Story Analysis
I pages Author's Note, p. 46	Groups of four students—each does one per week; group's work is collected and evaluated	Word cycle, p. 73	Listing ideas, choose five, p. 104	Character quotes, p. 52	What's in a chapter? p. 95
II p. 47–116		Create two spindlegrams using words from this week's reading	Be a Friend, p. 99	Their favorite things, p. 55	Extra, extra, read all about it, p. 84

RESPONSIBILITIES

Individual

- Read *Sounder* daily until finished
- Four I-prompt journal entries, one after each reading session
- Complete one piece of Team Work each week (two total for each person)
- Write one Higher-Order question each day in journal for discussion purposes

Team

- Team contracts and proposals due March 10
- Prepare and present team project
- Group project rubric for evaluation group
- Gather and turn in Team's Work

Figure 6–1. Group contract rotation

contracting and the variety and choice–and they *produced* happily. Doug just stretched their zones a bit too far.

The first example (see Appendix, pp. 116 and 117) may overemphasize the nonnegotiable side. I'd need to examine the *packs*, but my suspicion is that they are a bit too much of the one-size-fits-all variety. However, Doug knows his children and I don't—I drop in occasionally and he is with them every day, and he

Group Project Rubric

Team Name: _____ Date: _____

Topic: _____

Check one type of assessment:

Self _____   Group _____   Teacher_____

1. Criterion _____

1	2	3	4	5
Smattering of Applause		Round of Applause		Standing Ovation

2. Criterion _____

1	2	3	4	5
Smattering of Applause		Round of Applause		Standing Ovation

3. Criterion _____

1	2	3	4	5
Smattering of Applause		Round of Applause		Standing Ovation

4. Criterion _____

1	2	3	4	5
Smattering of Applause		Round of Applause		Standing Ovation

Figure 6–2. Adapted rubric for grade six group project

knows their thresholds. Notice, too, the nonnegotiable how-to lessons and discussions that are built in—good signs that there is not too much individual, lower
order work. Additionally, self-checking is evident. Even better is the self-evaluation page—Doug involves his students in reflection nicely here. His menu, as with
Biff's, needs to be expanded over time—you see the influence of my samples from
my earlier contracting days. Doug has borrowed and adapted, and I'm sure that
the menu will evolve gradually as he and his students take risks and grow.

The next contract that Doug developed was shorter in duration and almost
totally nonnegotiable. The lack of choice and heavy emphasis on packs and skill

work apparently did contribute to contract overload for his kids. A later contract from Doug, after he gave the group a few weeks off, was much more successful, as the students were happy with the negotiable possibilities.

The samples of contracts presented in this book are only the proverbial tip of the iceberg. Contracts allow the teacher to customize depending on local curricular, adopted material and standards to be measured—but, more importantly, they allow response based on teacher and student predilections, needs, thresholds, and curiosities.

This little book should provide you with the impetus to experiment, take risks, and listen to kids in the middle. They know what they need. Bon voyage!

7

Practicalities for Earlier Grades

And gladly wolde he lerne and gladly teche.
—GEOFFREY CHAUCER
Prologue, *The Canterbury Tales*

Although the purview for this book has been pretty much focused on grades 4 through 9, I can share some applications to younger children. All of what you'll find in this chapter is quite adaptable; if you have a heterogeneous fifth grade class, for example, you're likely to have a range from around third to seventh grade *skills* in terms of readability, not to mention a wider range (probably) in motivation, work habits, and interests. Here are some practicalities with the earlier grades.

New Zealand

A few years ago, while on sabbatical, I took advantage of the interim between semesters of graduate study and spent a month in New Zealand. In between a fishing trip on the Bay of Islands and motoring around the North Island, I made a concerted effort to connect with teachers (I was unable to visit in schools, as January is summertime down under). I met several teachers in my travels, and we were able to compare notes over pints of Steinlager and DB.

I got a variety of perspectives on curriculum, reading recovery, and methods of teaching reading that align with the natural ways in which children learn. I also had great conversations with a young teacher named Christine who taught seven and eight year olds and made extensive use of contracts. Here are some of her thoughts and pointers:

- Tasks should not be set readings or workbook pages, rather they should be experiments, written work, and points where reference to the teacher are helpful.
- She saw contract time as good time to alter teaching spaces, particularly including learning centers.
- Once her children were ready, she would hold *choosing time* for about an hour a day, in a fashion similar to Tomlinson's *anchor activities*, as a way to segue to greater choice (see Appendix, p. 119). Each child has the same contract, but he or she is free to choose the order in which the activities are done.
- She'd buttress choosing time with a *class contract*, which is essentially what Atwell (1987) would call a "status of the class" device. The choosing time options are listed on one axis, and kids' names are listed on the other. As I recall, Christine filled it in earlier in the year, but turned the responsibility over to the children as the year went on.
- She also mentioned a *skill contract* (see Appendix, p. 120) and supplied some examples. Even young children were involved in self-assessment, although she did grade them as necessary.
- She was very pleased with the way contracts allowed her to hold conferences and attend to individual needs while the rest of the class knew exactly what to do—she used the term "get on with it." To keep track of what students were doing, she created some engaging visuals (see Appendix, p. 121).
- She talked about the necessity for *gradual release of control* that I had found necessary with older children—she said that everyone always has something to do, even the most able.

Penelope

I also have spent time working with a contracting practitioner in an integrated second grade. Penny is a high-energy, conscientious mid-career teacher. Here are her tips:

- For the first five weeks she has to tell them exactly what it's all about.
- Early on, the students must feel secure; get used to her standards and routines; and, understand the need for independence.
- She says that kids get engrossed in what they're doing and care enough to get it right. She said that she has no behavior problems whatsoever because all of her kids are succeeding.
- She talked repeatedly about the opportunity to "sit and talk" with kids— she says, "You've got to know the children." She expressed concern about

young and inexperienced teachers being able to manage everything properly, for it's "a lot of documentation."

- She talked about the "right atmosphere where no one feels threatened" and, as Christine had, the need for gradual release to students. She said, "I could never start 'til I know the children and their abilities!"

Kathy

I worked with Kathy in my capacity at the time as a reading specialist. At the time we were contracting, she was teaching third grade.

Kathy was kind and her class was structured and child centered, yet quite demanding. She shares some of her tips.

- Third graders need the contracts as boundaries for what they can do. They feel safer when they know exactly what's expected of them. They *want* the boundaries.
- Her children who exhibited short attention spans when she instructed traditionally exhibited improved capacity to attend under contracting parameters—she marveled at this.
- She found contracting to be "more wearing" on the teacher, but felt that the tradeoff in increased student productivity and improved behavior was well worth it.
- She also expressed concerns about keeping track and evaluations for new teachers—I found this interesting because she was quite new at the time. She stated that it was easy for a child to disappear or fake it for awhile if the teacher was not vigilant.

Donna

Donna teaches fourth grade and is innovative and upbeat, and her approach is child centered. She mixes and matches commercial material with her own products and processes.

She has her students on contracts for different patterns in terms of time—she may do one week on the calendar, but only for the morning language arts block on Monday, Wednesday, and Friday. Another contract will be for a month of Thursdays. Some of her comments follow:

- Every methodology has its drawbacks, but this one has the fewest.
- Kids love the contracting time; I love contracts too. There's a temptation to do them too much. I need to be careful not to burn kids out.
- I feel that I'm teaching each child. Before contracts, as hard as I tried, I didn't do a good job of challenging the high-end kids.

Donna talked about the need to "start smaller" with younger students—she had examined some sixth grade contracts that were pretty far along in terms of student independence and felt that it would be too risky to go there with her own students. There is no magical formula, just good common sense, when contracting with younger children. In capsule form, my reminders are as follows:

- Don't sell them short.
- Start very small, move quite incrementally, but move, from one anchor activity, to two.
- Take advantage of self-contained situations, and possibilities for integration.

- Remember scaffolding needs and opportunities; be concrete.
- Experiment to find the best fit for you and your class.

Jane

Jane is a fourth grade teacher, in the same district as Kathy. I worked with her on contracting with both third and fourth grade children. Jane is one of those special teachers who laugh a lot and enjoy their kids—and at the same time treats learning as serious business. She is structured, yet flexible. The toughest, neediest children were often assigned to her, and she helped many young learners find themselves. Here is a contract that she developed for her fourth graders (see Appendix, p. 122). It extends for two weeks, and includes a menu. Under number 5, "write a letter as Clifford," her fourth graders were involved with a buddy program that paired them with first graders in their building. They read the Norman Bridwell books with their buddies, and they did a lot of writing as incognito Cliffords. As a culminating activity, there was an assembly when Clifford (one of the reading specialists, in drag in a costume from Scholastic . . . guess who filled the costume?) appeared, handed out special awards, and danced a bit.

Integration and Interdisciplinarity

The teachers who've been profiled were in self-contained situations. Before they began contracting, they had all been doing good, sound instructional things with children. Once they started learning how to best take advantage of the possibilities of contracts, things jelled for them even better.

Kids at the younger end of the continuum do not *crave* independence as much as early adolescents. As was mentioned earlier, in fact, they need safety and structure—yet at the same time they want to try out new things, take some risks, and be creative. I'll simply remind you to know your children well, yet don't be afraid to challenge them. Remember that contracts can be used to buttress and enhance (and especially to marry, to connect) existing structures and methodologies (e.g., workshops, literature circles, SSR, cooperative learning) and to take the ceiling off for many of your students.

It should be apparent that there is absolutely no one way, no single path with contract learning. *Adaptability* is the watchword.

8

Pulling It All Together

When dealing with people, let us remember we are not dealing with creatures of logic.
We are dealing with creatures of emotion, creatures bristling with prejudices
and motivated by pride and vanity.

—DALE CARNEGIE

As I pull things together in this chapter, I will exhort and plead alternately. Learning contracts can truly change the world of work for converts who find them to match their own teaching styles and the learning needs of their students.

I'll start with some real voices. The first voice is that of Ryan, a junior education major at a local university. Ryan was a *turned off* learner until very recently. His professor incorporated some contracting components into his language arts course and caught Ryan at the right time in his development. The opportunity, at age twenty, to choose certain aspects of his curriculum evoked some strong (and at times unpleasant) memories of his own middle school experiences. I choose to include Ryan's learning log both for its wry commentary on middle school learning as well as the fact that Ryan was able to communicate freely in the choice-driven, student-centered culture that he rarely experienced in his previous years of schooling:

Although I always did well in school, I would definitely consider myself a *resistant learner*. All students start out loving school as children, but as they get older and begin to formulate their own opinions, school can become more of a hassle than anything else. "Research tells us that, in general, attitudes about reading, writing, and school decline steadily through the elementary years and become particularly negative in the intermediate and middle grades" (Worthy 2000, 299). This quote seems logical to me as I recall the record seventeen times I skipped school in sixth grade. My motivation for my consistent "hooky playing," as my mom calls it,

79

stemmed not only by the fact that I was not challenged in school, but also because I had an older brother who was in eighth grade and who was probably not the best influence on me at that time.

Jo Worthy makes an outstanding point, when she describes how the interests of the middle level students do not match the curriculum. Throughout my schooling I cannot remember one teacher who ever inquired about my interests and my hobbies. As a result, I would always be the first one done assignments and then I would be that brat in the back of the classroom asking, "When will I ever use this in real life." Even though my work was complete and correct, my heart really wasn't in it. I did enough to get the grades that I desired and that was it. My middle school years, much like everyone else I know, was a time of turmoil. I was forming my own opinions about social issues, and many other things, including school. I was not challenged, and I was not known in the least by any adults.

Middle level students are growing up and with that they are longing for freedom and independence. These characteristics of independence, freedom, and choice should be mirrored in the curriculum. At this age, students no longer want to be told what to do. If students are told what to do, they will rebel and no matter what is done from that point on will be in vain, because the students will not relate to the material and they will not care about their own learning; The key words, I think, are choice and flexibility. It is important to allow the students to explore their learning and explore their interests because it allows them to have ownership over their own learning; some will still probably say they hate school, but your mission will be accomplished. Worthy writes, "In my experience, students are more motivated to learn when educators listen to their interests and provide choices in instruction" (299). We as teachers need to get off our high horse and allow the students to control the curriculum and the instruction, not vice versa. I can't wait to get my chance to open my students' eyes to their own knowledge and learning.

Ryan remembers his early adolescent years as stultifying and infantilizing. Yet he was able to still get good grades—partly because he was bright, and largely because the curriculum was unchallenging.

As part of his contract in the university language arts class, his professor supplied Ryan with a manila folder filled with articles, brochures, and the like that were tailored to the young man's interests and likes. (Ryan was particularly interested in poetry, which the professor found a bit incongruous for a young man who had had legal scrapes and also had a pretty tough, street-wise veneer. Yet his poetic proclivity was apparent, so the teacher took a chance on Linda Rief and portfolio issues, figuring that that might strike a responsive chord. The article was "Sarah: Speaking for Herself" in the November 1996 issue of *Voices from the Middle*.) The following is Ryan's closing journal entry for the course:

The Manila Folder

"Stay the course." That's what you said to me about a week ago. That statement really touched me. It showed me that you are really concerned and that you are really pulling for me. For that I thank you . . . you didn't have to take the time to put together that folder full of stuff. The most influential that you gave me was definitely the article about Sarah. The article completely blew me away. On one hand I couldn't believe the level of work and reflection that this fourteen year old produced. On the other hand, I began to feel a little bit bad about the portfolio I'm about to turn in. . . . The piece on Sarah has served as a beacon of hope that I will someday be able to inspire, not similar, but relatively good work from my students . . . I thank you again and want you to know how much you helped me.

Even twenty year olds respond to teachers who know them and care about them. In a classroom community, barriers are broken down.

More on Differentiation from the Literature

I respectfully disagree with Winebrenner's (1992) limitation of contracts to applications solely for the gifted and talented. I prefer to think that contracts bring out

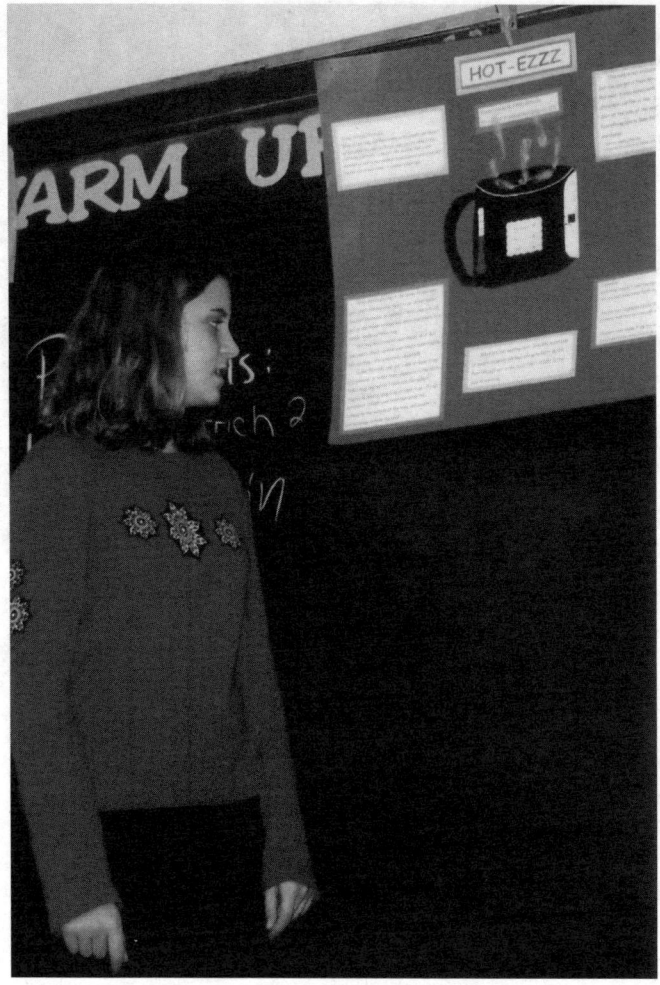

the opportunity to develop the gifts and talents of all children, particularly at this stage. As mentioned previously, early adolescents are like crustaceans shedding their shells, and like crustaceans, they are most vulnerable at this life stage.

As opposed to proponents of gifted-only contracts, we are reminded by Carol Tomlinson (1999) that schools must belong to all children. We must rethink *how* we do school, in addition to considering for *whom*. Tomlinson states that there is no one "right way" to deliver an effectively differentiated classroom, that teachers who practice differentiation are "students of their students," (2) who begin where students are, not on the first page of the curriculum guide.

She goes on to debunk the theory that by simply creating heterogeneous classes we will provide equity and excellence for all learners. Tomlinson states that "heterogeneity usually is a one-size-fits-all endeavor where the learning plan swallows some learners and pinches others. Such classes provide neither equity [nor] excellence" (22).

Mere heterogeneity, as it is typically practiced, misses the proverbial boat for the range of learners. Advanced learners are often viewed as fine without special provisions because they are already "up to standard." Worse, they are often expected to serve as peer coaches or otherwise wait (patiently, of course, says Tomlinson) while their classmates continue to work for mastery. Additionally, struggling learners will not de facto catch up by being grouped heterogeneously. As much as the rhetoric claims the need for higher expectations, the mere fact that the bar is raised does not ensure that learning will be enhanced. As Tomlinson put it so aptly, "Struggling learners will not experience more long-term success in heterogeneous classes unless we are ready and able to meet them at their points of readiness and systematically escalate their learning until they are able to function as competently and confidently as other learners" (1999, 22). Finally, there is no such thing as an average learner in the fourth through ninth grade bracket. Kids who are labeled by being unlabeled, those regular, average, typical, ordinary, unremarkable students who make up the majority of our classes, have a huge range of predilections, skills, wants, and needs that are being blatantly ignored—until we consciously build effective communities of learners in which the needs of all children are specifically and consistently attended to.

Tomlinson (1993, 1999) elaborates on contracting as a means to the end product/process of student responsiveness. She reminds us that "developing classrooms that actively attend to both student similarities and student differences is anything but simple" (1999, 8). She exhorts teachers to be reflective practitioners, to examine their philosophies about individual needs. Teachers must know themselves in order to grow and evolve in order to (primarily) build learning communities for the children's sake, as well as to (secondarily) feel more confident and comfortable in fielding questions from peers, parents, and the public. She also reminds teachers of the need to talk with students early and often, providing a continuous feedback loop.

She is clear that both principals and teachers must think it's worth the trouble to create differentiated classes. "Change is complex, messy, and unpredictable. When we undertake change we start, we start over, and we even skip steps" (Tomlinson 1999, 109). Staff development needs to be ongoing and leadership needs to be excellent if teachers are truly going to move away from teach-to-the-middle instruction. When individuals who are growing meet opposition, they are quick to revert back to the known and secure (Sparks and Hirsh 1997).

Fifth and Sixth Grade Visits

My purpose was to spend some time visiting teachers and students practicing the art of contract learning. My intention was to gather some recent artifacts and to really probe a bit, to get opinions about learning contracts from students who were not my own.

I chose Beverly Tihansky's sixth graders at Nitschmann Middle School. To contextualize, Nitschmann is one of four middle schools in what can best be characterized as a "small urban/suburban" school system. The Bethlehem Area School District has about 14,000 students; approximately 35 percent are Hispanic or African American. The Nitschmann building demographics are more suburban, in that the feeding elementary schools are more white and middle class than the district at large.

Mrs. Tihansky teaches the children I observed for three fifty-minute periods daily: a double block of reading/language arts (which includes Junior Great Books as well as Philosophy for Children) and a single daily period of math. She has been using learning contracts for about twenty years.

The school building is of the 1930s vintage, but has been overhauled and modernized. It's quiet; I garner my visitor's badge in the office and head down the hall to Bev's room. She has a prep period before the kids' 10:20 arrival, and we talk and catch up. This is one vibrant, high-energy woman—now a grandmother, she loves her job and says so. I have brought some of my treasured samples of students' work and I talk a little about how I've tailored things in recent years. She shows me a few things on display—and then, with a wink, she says she'll pull out her recent "good stuff" from her adjacent storage area. It's a gold mine.

I vicariously feel her pride and excitement regarding the quality of her students' work. I dutifully try to focus in on one item for a while, but I keep on getting distracted by something else even more joyful and creative. Then kids come rolling in—thirty-two eleven and twelve year olds. They sit down, take out their stuff (Bev later explains that each child has five portfolios, all color coded) and she quickly, cordially greets them. Half of the class goes off to the library and the rest remain in the classroom. She introduces them to me; it happens to be "retro" day, and most are dressed in tie-dyed shirts and bell bottoms. I ask them to warm up with a five-to ten-minute free writing period about how they feel about contracting.

Bev and I talk quietly while they are writing. She has her children on contracts for ninety days in a year—that means all of the time possible/available, opposite the district mandated Junior Great Books and Philosophy for Children sessions. Bethlehem is firmly standards based and participates in the New Standards Consortium; Bev is sure to show me the rubrics that are posted on the walls and/or in designated areas for student access. She does have an anthology that she must make use of, and parts of her contracts are customized around the stories and activities contained therein.

As the free writing continues, some of the kids are winding up. A few go to a table to pick up laminated numbers (like we'd do in a delicatessen) and a few more open up folders and prepare to work. I remind them of my purpose, tell them that they can be totally honest about the good, the bad, and the ugly. Then I listen and take notes as they talk.

There is a flurry of hand raising and talk as they proffer opinions, nod, and build on each other's thoughts and opinions. Some things that were said to the general question of plusses and minuses follow:

Negatives
- The first one was a "little overwhelming."
- They had to learn to "pace themselves" (but admitted that that was a plus, too).
- The contracts can be "very time consuming"; it's a big mistake not to keep up, or to procrastinate.

Positives

- Contracts teach us time management and responsibility.
- They are "fun" (said repeatedly).
- We get to choose (said repeatedly).
- We get to be creative (said repeatedly).
- We get what we earn; we're not obligated to work for As, but we know how to figure out how to get the grades we want.

They tell me that they have plenty of opportunities for group work and excitedly invite me back to see their "performances," which they do at the end of each contract (they are just starting a four week long contract). I ask them to tell me a little about how they use technology and I query them on what their parents would tell me about contracts if they were present.

- One girl said that her mother "learned a lot" by helping with her project.
- A couple commented that their parents said it was a lot of work (i.e., for their kids), sometimes, and on the weekends in particular.
- They show me examples of how they use the internet for their research, and specific software for design and creativity.
- Back to the parent thing, I remember a few problems with my seventh graders when parents would "borrow" my kids' SSR books, get hooked, and kids would not have access to the books.

After the question and answer period, the kids settle into their work. Bev says she'd talk to me after she's met quickly with each student. Then she calls, "Number one" and Jackie comes up with her work to be checked and a project to turn in. After a two-minute miniconference, Bev says, "Number two" and the next child quickly appears, work in hand. Bev tells me later that she doesn't want to "waste any time; can't afford to" and with a smile relates that she got the pick a number idea while waiting in line at the delicatesson one day.

She spends a few minutes, or less, with each of the nine kids that take a number, then we talk a bit more. I've been watching the kids working. I ask Bev what her biggest tips to other teachers would be. As we talk, I marvel (yet am not surprised at all) at the fact that she can focus totally on me without having to manage the class at all for a chunk of time. Her thoughts for contracting teachers are:

- Save examples, attach them to the rubrics; kids love to see good work and to do even better.
- Hold kids back once in a while; don't let them work too hard. She says that her class "begged" her to give them this particular contract before Christmas

vacation so that they could get started on it, and that she refused. The same thing happens on weekends—she is *public* with them about not giving them their new contracts on a Friday so that they'll take the weekends off.

I talk to her about how she handles the correction load. She says she'd be "insane" to even attempt to correct or respond to all of their work. She says that she has them correct a lot of their own work, and that she does a lot with peer response as well.

We talk on about the kids and the quality work they produce. I remark that her contract documents themselves are lengthier, more specific, and more explicit regarding point values than the ones I do with seventh graders. She says that sixth graders need "more structure." I wander around, admiring and fussing over what they have produced. These kids are natural, comfortable, and happy. The literature on motivation is consistent (Gambrell and Morrow 1995) in documenting how so many students turn off literacy as they progress from the early elementary grades through the middle level. These children, however, see themselves as readers and writers and thinkers and creators of quality products.

Written Comments from Children and Adults

As I reflect back on Nitschmann, it occurs to me how eager to please kids still are—when they have some control. Mrs. Tihansky is tough and demanding. She does not use terms like *zone of proximal development* and *community of learners*. She does talk about young people who "work hard," "get along," and "are organized and responsible."

Her comments, emailed to me recently, follow:

As opposed to the earlier questions that she answered off the cuff, I wanted her to take time to write me short answers to four questions:

1. Why contracting?
2. Advantages?
3. Disadvantages?
4. Do they fit with the standards movement?

Do you remember how I commented that she doesn't waste any time in the classroom? Her efficiency and energy are palpable in her email:

Scott,

Finally arrived home, safe and sound. Back into the swing of things after just one day. Decided to get an answer off to you before I get involved with report card grades. Here goes:

1. *Why contracting?* Meet with kids more on a 1 to 1 basis, better handle on individual strengths and weaknesses, creativity is shared more consistently, competition is enhanced in a positive atmosphere, no time wasted, kids have an interest in learning and doing well, many opportunities to improve writing skills and students choose activities they have an interest in.

2. *Advantages?* Very manageable, interesting to students and teacher alike, well defined expectations, students take responsibility for their own grade based on effort, teacher available to help those who need help, group projects possible with planning time built in, clever and creative results, and contracts create a working classroom where the "me" is replaced by "we."

3. *Disadvantages?* Initial writing of written agreement, parent complaints due to expectations and work involved that interferes with family time, time constraints, and time management skills of students.

4. *Fit with standards?* Absolutely! Rewritten constantly to parallel standards . . . ex. this year I included a persuasive writing piece to go along with a story and the creative presentations certainly revolve around rubrics and standards.

Hope this helps. Kids are all excited that you have an interest in what they are doing. This Friday and Monday we will be doing presentations if you are free to join us. They can also repeat them for you on another day. Let me know. I will at least be able to get some pictures for you.

—*Bev*

Next we have a sampling of the quick writes that the sixth graders did on my first visit. They were simply asked to write about what they saw as the plusses and the minuses of contracting. I said that I and others were *wondering* about contract learning—Colin was amused by the term.

Dear Wonderers,

Contracts are great. I love them. They are so much fun. I encourage every student to do contracts. You may ask how will these help students in real life. I think the most important reason for contracts is because the contract gives children responsibilities. They also make you creative. The only problem that I can see is children don't get to do other things even though school is more important. Secondly, students who are lazy and wait 'til the last minute come across problems with contracts.

—*Colin Santoro*

The things that are good about contracts are that you are not obligated to do a certain amount of work. By judging the activities you decide if you want to do that certain activity. Because of the "point system" you basically decide your grade, because it depends how much work you are willing to do and how much effort you are willing to put forth.

Some disadvantages are that you sometimes feel obligated to work, but if you have an organized system of getting work done, and not leaving it all to the last minute, it is not as bad as it seems, or you make it seem.

Contracts also help you manage your time in an organized way because you have to manage your time so you can manage to get your goals met.

—*Jackie Dunne*

One thing that is good about contracts is they're fun. A lot of the activities are different from your average projects. For example: creating a survival product, designing a CD cover, and making a Now and Then poster. The only bad thing about contracts is they take up all your time. You're supposed to have fun on weekends, right. Well when I have a contract, I can't have fun because I'm so BUSY! Overall, contracts are fun and they are great to have!

—*Caitlin Worrich*

Some advantages we have while doing contracts is we are able to do only the things that we want to do. At the end, we only have to do what we choose and get the grade that we want to get. We have to motivate ourselves because Mrs. Tihansky doesn't push us to a point to get an A or an A+. It is like choosing our own grade. We have to manage our time and motivate ourselves to do a certain amount of work.

To start out, there aren't many disadvantages when we do contracts. One disadvantage is you are not pushed by your teacher. It is your own motivation. If you are lazy you won't get anywhere.

—*Divya Chalikonda*

The thing I love about contracts is that you get to decide how many points you want to get to determine your grade. Like on some other project you wouldn't get to pick your grade but on contracts it's different. I really like contracts and if I ever became a teacher I would do them.

The bad thing about contracts is that sometimes I have a hard time getting everything done to get the grade I want by the due date. There is a lot of work to do to get an A.

— *Bridget Cunningham*

It's a very brisk February morning as I walk down the hill from the district office to E. T. Richardson Middle School in Springfield, PA. I have arranged to spend the morning with three contracting teachers and their classes, two fifth grades and a sixth. I have some concerns about too many packets and worksheets being built in to the contracts, for these teachers have all been instructed by district management to "teach the program" (i.e., do the subskills); lots of district dollars were spent recently on a commercial *program*, in response to a community/school board demand for more consistency. I have recently heard Dr. Jean Paratore of Boston University remind teachers that a minimum of 50 percent of the language arts block should be devoted to whole acts (i.e., extended, connected immersion) of reading and writing. The Richardson teachers are in a bit of a bind, but I am hopeful that they will thoughtfully, gradually lessen the volume rather than completely cease and desist. Kids do need variety, and they do need skills.

I go to each class, spend a few minutes cruising the rooms and watching the children work, and then randomly take five to seven students aside from each class to write and talk about how things are going. Those chosen are very excited to give their feedback. I tell them to tell all—the good, the bad, and the ugly. But first I have each group do some free writing, simply telling what is good about contract learning and what could be improved. Some common trends are apparent, first from a summation of these students' interview comments.

The Good

- Contracts teach us responsibility.
- We don't have to wait; we have control of time.
- We have to keep organized.
- We have variety.
- Sometimes we have choices.
- We like contract time better than teacher-led lessons.
- The time goes fast; we get involved (regular lessons can get boring).
- We can earn good grades.
- We like projects; we like negotiables.
- We like partnering, but sometimes one kid does too much of the work.
- Our teacher listens to us, respects us.

The Bad

- The contract we just did was too hard, too much work.
- We don't like the worksheets—they are boring, some are too hard.

A few of the kids' written comments follow:

The thing I like about contracts is that we can go and do it in any order like top to bottom or something like that. I also like that you have to sign it so you promise to finish all the work.

One thing I don't like about it is that some things are not as fun as others and they take a little longer but I still like the contract. I would say that the contract is great.

—*Kerry Reis, grade 5*

I think contracts are great because you get a couple assignments all at the same time and you know when there [sic] going to be due. Contracts also make you feel more responsible for your work. The other good thing is when you sign the contract your [sic] promising to get the work done on time.

The only thing I don't like about contracts is that there [sic] usually worth a lot of points toward your grade.

—*Karen Woods, grade 5*

What I like about contracts is how we get to pick and choose some activities that we want to do. I also like doing the projects. The things I dislike about contracts is that sometimes their [sic] too long and sometimes their [sic] too short. If their [sic] were fifteen things on the contract it would take me about eleven days to finish. If the fifteenth thing were projects. If the fifteen things were just worksheets, it would only take me about five days. Some contracts you have to rush through, that is why you need more time sometimes. Overall I think I like contracts but you just need time to do them.

—*Amelia Washington, grade 5*

The teachers of the fifth graders were new to contracting. Amelia's comment about "sometimes long, sometimes short" can present a problem. It's one of the risks these teachers took as they chose to stretch themselves out of their own zones. The contracts that these fifth graders were working on are included. Teachers Madeleine O'Dowd and Alicia Kalbach (see Appendix, pp. 123–125) both used contracts to build stamina and capacity gradually. I really admired the E. T. Richardson teachers, for they undertook the rigors of contract management and setup on top of the exigencies of learning the aforementioned new district-adopted language arts program.

Sixth grade teacher Denise Mroz had been contracting for several years. Her written comments follow:

I have been using contracts for several years. As a teacher I have seen many positive aspects. My students also enjoy using them.

Contracts are student friendly. They allow children to work at their own pace with freedom of choice and responsibility of their own education. Students like feeling in control. Contracts also enable them to learn how to manage their own time and learn their learning styles.

As a teacher, I enjoy my classroom during contracts. The students are in charge of decision making, time management and they enjoy making their own decisions.

They can take a quiz or an assessment when they are ready, not on the designated day I choose. I could not imagine teaching without using contracts.

The free writing of two of Denise's sixth graders follow. There were occasional complaints about too many practice book pages (remember the district mandate for consistency), but for the most part the students were producing happily and willingly:

I like the way we do the contracts. I like being able to look at the packet to see what I have to do next. I wouldn't change it. I like taking the tests on my own. It shows us that we have responsibility. If we forget that's our problem. We are old enough to do it on our own. Besides, it might help us in the future. That's why I don't think we should change it and leave it the way it is.

—*Ashley Taylor, grade 6*

I like using contracts on our stories. It not only keeps me on task but it tells me and reminds me what to do. The only thing I would change would be the strategy sheets like the fish bones they are hard. I would change the number of facts down to six instead of eight. That's what I would change or fix.

—*Becca Davison, grade 6*

It's a Wrap

Look at Figure 8–1, "Portrait of a Thirteen Year Old." I've used this as an over-head for a variety of presentations over the years. It's a reminder of the awesome range that middle school teachers face each day. We really must embrace the diversity of this stage, revel in it, wallow in it, celebrate it—yet not sweat it. Just because a child is in, say, seventh grade, he or she can is not be tidily compart-mentalized and ready, willing, or able to take on *grade level* work. Those of us who have taught anywhere in the broad middle level band know of these types, who often sat side by side, and at times were possibly even embodied in the same young person. The mysterious, emerging *I* is captured in a remarkable poem, penned by twelve-year-old Caroline on page 94.

---

6 feet 2 inches——4 feet 7 inches
trips going up stairs ——Olympics gold medal winner
alcoholic, drug addict——Sunday school leader, little leaguer
wears braces, has zits——competes in Teenage Miss America
turned off, preparing to quit school——curious and enthusiastic learner
has trouble with whole numbers——ready for trigonometry
a regular in juvenile court——an eagle scout
already a mother of two——plays with dolls
unable to read the comics——enjoys Dickens novels

Source: The Essential Middle School

Figure 8–1. Portrait of a thirteen year old

Middle School Anxiety
by Caroline Smith

I know the real me's in there
  Far down in my heart
But the only thing you glimpse
  Is a tiny, little part

What people actually see,
  Is not what is inside
I'm scared of what they'll find
  And so I simply hide

Somedays I'm a cheerful girl,
  Others a confused child
Sometimes I seem to be serious
  Sometimes a little wild

Few have ever seen me cry,
  Though many have seen a dimple
But sometimes I have to ask myself
  "Why can't life be simple?"

So one day, when you're passing by,
  And don't recognize what you see
The somebody who you're looking at,
  Is really only me.

If you are just starting your journey toward child-centered teaching, be strong, be consistent in matching your practices with your philosophy. If you are a bit farther along, looking for growth and challenge and better ways to help kids, I urge you to sustain yourself and keep on reflecting and tinkering.

I referred to contracting earlier as a structure, a tool that can help to enable differentiation of instruction and other child-centered practices. I do not offer contracting as the only way to achieve differentiated classrooms. I simply feel that contracting merits more prominence due to all of the flexibility and potential for meeting kids' needs. Schools must encourage students to take responsibility for regulating their own learning, for being self-determining and autonomous. Students rarely persist in attempting to learn skills that may not interest them and have no apparent value to them.

I urge you to look closely at contracting as a tool for differentiation that increases student engagement. When I said to Ryan "Stay the course," I would certainly have forgotten my own words, had he not repeated them for me. I urge you, too, to find your course, and, yes, stay the course!

References

Anderson, Richard, Elfrieda Hiebert, Judith Scott, and Ian Anderson. 1985. *Becoming a Nation of Readers: The Report of the Commission on Reading*. Champaign, IL: Center for the Study of Reading, University of Illinois.

Atwell, Nancie. 1987, 1999. *In the Middle: Writing, Reading, and Learning with Adolescents*. Portsmouth, NH: Heinemann.

Beane, James. 1990. *A Middle School Curriculum: From Rhetoric to Reality*. Columbus, OH: National Middle School Association.

Boomer, Garth, (ed). 1983. *Writing with Power: Exploratory People*. National Conference of Australian Association of Teaching English.

Brimfield, Renee, Frank Masci, and Denise DeFiore. 2002. "Differentiating Instruction to Teach All Learners." *Middle School Journal* 33: 14–18.

Buckner, Aimee. 2002. "Teaching in a World Focused on Testing." *Language Arts* 79: 212–215.

Burns, Deborah. 2002. "Standards and Curriculum Differentiation." *Education Update* 44: 3.

Carnegie Council on Adolescent Development. 1989. *Turning Points: Preparing American Youth for the 21st Century*. Washington, DC: Carnegie Corporation.

Dudley-Marling, Curt, and Sharon Murphy. 2001. "Changing the Way We Think About Language Arts." *Language Arts* 78: 574–578.

Erikson, Eric. 1963. *Childhood and Society* (2nd ed.). New York: Norton.

Fielding, Linda, and P. David Pearson. 1994. "Reading Comprehension: What Works?" *Educational Leadership* 51.5: 62–67.

Fulwiler, Toby. 1978. "Journal Writing Across the Curriculum." Paper presented at the annual meeting of Conference on College Composition and Communication. ERIC Ed. 161073: 2&4.

Gallagher-Polite, Mary. 2001. "From Turning Points to Transformation Points: A Reinvention Paradigm for Middle Schools." *Middle School Journal* 33: 21–27.

Gambrell, Linda, and Leslie M. Morrow. 1995. "Creating Motivating Contexts for Literacy Learning." In Lawrence Baker, Peter Afflerbach, and Donald Reinking (eds.), *Developing Engaged Readers in Home and School Communities* (pp. 115–136). Mahwah, NJ: Erlbaum.

Greenwood, Scott C. 1995. "Learning Contracts and Transaction: A Natural Marriage in the Middle." *Language Arts*, 72: 88–96.

Greenwood, Scott C. 1989. "Summary, Compare, Contrast, and Critique: Encouraging Active Reading Through the Use of Cinema." *Exercise Exchange* 35: 22–24.

Greenwood, Scott C. 1985. "Use of Contracts to Motivate and Manage your Secondary Reading Class." *Journal of Reading*, 28: 487–491.

Hodgkinson, Harold. 1992. "Reform Versus Reality." *Phi Delta Kappan* 73: 9–16.

Hoffman, James V. 1992. "Leadership in the Language Arts: Am I Whole Yet? Are You?" *Language Arts* 69: 366–371.

Kaufman, Douglas. 2001. "Organizing and Managing the Language Arts Workshop: A Matter of Motion." *Language Arts* 79: 114–123.

Kilgore, Karen, Cynthia Griffin, Paul Sindelar, and Rodman Webb. 2002. "Restructuring for Inclusion: Changing Teaching Practices (Part II)." *Middle School Journal* 33: 7–13.

Ohanion, Susan. 1999. *One Size Fits Few: The Folly of Educational Standards*. Portsmouth, NH: Heinemann.

Parkhurst, Helen. 1922 *Education on the Dalton Plan*. London: Bell.

Pitton, Debra. 2001. "The School and the Child and the Child in the School." *Middle School Journal* 33: 14–20.

Popham, James. 2001. "Teaching to the Test?" *Educational Leadership* 58: 16–20.

Rief, Linda, and Sarah Jasinski. 1996. "Sarah: Speaking for Herself." *Voices from the Middle* 3: 32–42.

Rief, Linda. 1992. *Seeking Diversity*. Portsmouth, NH: Heinemann.

Sparks, Dennis, and Stephanie Hirsh. 1997. *A New Vision for Staff Development*. Alexandria, VA: Association for Supervision and Curriculum Development.

Strackbein, Deanna, and Montague Tillman. 1987. "The Joy of Journals—with Reservations." *Journal of Reading* 31: 28–31.

Tierny, Robert, and John Readence. 2000. *Reading Strategies and Practices: A Compendium*. (5th ed.). Boston: Allyn and Bacon.

Tomlinson, Carol Ann. 1999. *The Differentiated Classroom: Responding to the Needs of All Learners*. Alexandria, VA: Association for Supervision and Curriculum Development.

Tomlinson, Carol Ann. 1995. *How to Differentiate Instruction in Mixed-Ability Classrooms*. Alexandria, VA: Association for Supervision and Curriculum Development.

Tomlinson, Carol Ann. 1993. "Independent Study: A Flexible Tool for Encouraging Academic and Personal Growth." *Middle School Journal*, 25: 55–59.

Tracy, Saundra, and Scott C. Greenwood. 1991. "Search for Identity: Middle School Educators and Staff Development." *American Middle School Education* 14: 3–12.

Vatterott, Cathy. 1995. "Student-Focused Instruction: Balancing Limits with Freedom in the Middle Grades." *Middle School Journal*, 25: 28–38.

Wiles, Jon, and Joseph Bondi. 1988. *The Essential Middle School.* Tampa, FL: Wiles, Bondi & Associates.

Winebrenner, Susan. 1992. *Teaching Gifted Children in the Regular Classroom.* Minneapolis, MN: Free Spirit Press.

White, George P., and Scott C. Greenwood. 1992. "Using Learning Contracts to Empower Middle Level Students." *Middle School Journal* 23: 15–20.

Worthy, Jo. 2000. "Conducting Research on Topics of Student Interest." *The Reading Teacher* 54: 288–289.

Yair, Gerald. 2000. "Reforming Motivation: How the Structure of Instruction Affects Students' Learning Experiences." *British Educational Journal* 26: 191–210.

Zemelman, Steven, Harvey Daniels, and Arthur Hyde. 1998. *Best Practice: New Standards for Teaching and Learning in America's Schools* (2nd ed.). Portsmouth, NH: Heinemann.

Appendix

- Developmental Reading Contract 1
- 7-R Contract 1
- Menu: Negotiables
- Literature Extension Enterprise Evaluation
- Movie Summary and Critique Guidelines
- Guidelines: Summary, Critique, Compare, and Contrast (Book and Movie Comparison)
- Sample Letter to Parents
- Largely Negotiable Contract—Later in School Year
- Survival Unit Contract
- Menu List for Survival Unit
- Group Rotation for Survival Contract
- Reader's Workshop Contract
- Grade Six Menu Example
- Example of Grade Six Partner Contract
- *Sounder* Contract—Group Example
- Group Reading Project Menu
- Grade Six, One Week, Two-Hour Blocks Daily Learning Contract
- Choosing Time Contract
- Skill Contract
- Weekly Plan
- Fourth Grade Contract
- Fifth Grade Contract 1
- Fifth Grade Contract 2

Developmental Reading Contract 1

I, _____, being of sound mind and body, do hereby agree to complete the following tasks. I understand that more flexible contracts with more student choices will follow this year, if I do a good job on this one.

      A. SSR: (title) _____
      B. SSR extension of my choice: _____
      C. Five dialogue journal pages
      D. Crossword puzzle Set I
      E. Collage on lyrics of a song or poetry
      F. Student choice: _____

I understand that this contract is worth 125 points toward my first quarter grade. This contract has been explained to me, and I have seen samples of past students' work. I will self correct to the best of my ability and twelve-inch talk when appropriate.

(x) _____ (student)

I will continually offer guidance and help and prompt feedback so that students will achieve their best results.

(x) _____ (teacher)

(x) _____ (parent)

Early, structured contract

7-R Contract 1

I, _____, being of sound mind and body, do here-
by agree to stay "on task" at all times and to complete the following by Friday.

A. Nonnegotiable
Read SSR book _____
> Crossword set I
> Dialogue journal: 4 pages
> Categorization and eponyms, etc., handouts
> Anthology (2) 256-276 and quizzes
> Anthology packet 63-72 and self-correct

B. Negotiable (you choose)
1. Crossword set II
2. Original trivia questions and answers
3. Movie summary and critique
4. Collage: lyrics of song
5. Short story/or choose your own adventure
6. _____
7. _____

I understand this contract is worth 220 points and I will do my best work

(x) _____ (student)

I will render necessary services

(x) _____ (teacher)

I will support and monitor

(x) _____ (parent)

Partially negotiable contract

Menu: Negotiables

(x) _____

(Save all year)

1. Book summary and critique (oral, written or otherwise)
2. Move summary and critique
3. Magazine article summary and critique
4. Book and movie: summary, compare, contrast, and critique
5. Jamestown crossword puzzle sets
6. Word bank and/or word search
7. Original crossword based on self-selected reading book
8. Extra self-selected reading book(s) (extension of your choice)
9. Jamestown *Heroes/Disasters*
10. Journal writing beyond nonnegotiable
11. Collage: connotations of lyrics of song or poetry
12. Poetry about plus illustrations of emotions
13. Other original poetry
14. Author research
15. Other research: topic of interest
16. Original short story
17. Original choose your own adventure
18. Extra analogy sets
19. Original analogies
20. Original trivia questions and answers
21. _____
22. _____
23. _____
24. _____
25. _____

Seventh grade choices for negotiations

Literature Extension Group Evaluation

Name:_____   Date: _____

1. Written Component

Not Yet	Not Bad	Ah Hah!
*many spelling errors	*few spelling errors	*no spelling errors
*little evidence of story comprehension	*some evidence of comprehension	*story understanding is clear
*hard to read	*typed or written neatly	*presentation fully elaborated
*lacks flair, originality	*some voice, originality	*creative, has flair

2. Artwork

Out of the Gate	2nd Lap	Home Stretch
*no attention to detail	*some attention to detail	*fully detailed
*no evidence of careful planning	*some evidence of planning	*careful planning is obvious
*only one medium: no color	*1 or 2 media: some color	*many media used: fully colored

3. Spoken Piece

It's Greek to Me	The Fog is Lifting	Yes-Yes
*hard to hear	*adequate, but not enthusiastic	*good volume, expression
*unorganized	*logically sequenced	*organized the best way possible
*no eye contact w/audience	*some eye contact	*good interaction w/audience

4. Other _____

On the Bench	Rounding 2nd	Home Run!
*_____	*_____	*_____
*_____	*_____	*_____
*_____	*_____	*_____

Adapted rubric for group activity

Movie Summary and Critique Guidelines

First list: A) Title (underlined)
              B) Setting, time
              C) Main characters
              D) Rating (if known, if applicable)

Then, as in a book summary, tell me the main plot of your film–must be in sequence, must be clear; shouldn't be much more than two paragraphs.

Your final paragraph will be your critique—tell me why you did (or didn't) enjoy it, who you would recommend it to, whether you felt the rating was appropriate, etc.

Your final draft must reflect your best writing, and must bear the signature of at least one "proofer!"

(Side headings are a good idea.)

(The critique is what will make your paper unique.)

Example of guideline—stored in dump portfolio, activated for contract time

**Guidelines: Summary, Critique, Compare, and Contrast
(book and movie comparison)**

List: A) Title (both)
             B) Author (book)
             C) Type (book)
             D) Time and setting (both)
             E) Rating (of movie, if known)

Then write out:
Summary of both (main plot)

Compare and Contrast (major similarities and differences between book and movie versions)

Critique of both—which did you like better? Why? Deal with the movie rating, if appropriate—include a recommendation that is thoughtful

    √ Use side headings
    √ See example
    √ Rough draft, proofer's signature necessary

Another seventh grade guideline example

Dear Parents/Caretakers,

In seventh grade developmental reading class this year your child will learn and *practice* a wide array of skills and strategies to improve his or her reading. Your child will be practicing the whole act of reading both *assigned* materials and *self-selected* materials (books, movies, magazine articles, etc.), often under the parameters of a learning contract.

Seventh graders have a wide array of interests, backgrounds, and abilities. I will monitor their self-selection choices in partnership with you (you are your child's first and best teacher). Please be aware of what your child is viewing/writing/reading and contact me immediately if you have any questions or concerns.

Sincerely,

Scott C. Greenwood

Sample letter to parents

Contract 4

I, _____, still reasonably of sound mind and body, am ready for my fourth (and final!) contract of the year. I am thoroughly familiar with contract parameters.

Nonnegotiable

A) Self-selected reading (title) _____

B) Major writing process/product: _____

Negotiable (see menu for all of below)

A)

B)

C)

D)

E)

F)

*I understand that my self-selected reading book for this contract must come from the recommended reading list. I will negotiate for projects and activities that will show off my developing skills to their best advantage.

(x) _____ (student)
I will do my best work

(x) _____ (teacher)
I will continue to provide guidance and prompt feedback

(x) _____ (parent)
I will support as necessary

Largely negotiable contract—later in school year

Contract

I, _____ , do hereby agree to read

_____ written by _____.

I further agree to do the following activities during and upon completion of reading this book.

Nonnegotiable Activities
1. A character silhouette or character bag
2. An episode analysis

Negotiable Activities
1. From the menu list provided I will choose two story activities, one character activity, and one vocabulary activity.

Furthermore, once I have signed my contract, I realize I have only three school days to change any section of this contract. After the agreed date no changed can be made. I understand that I may meet with Miss Gray to discuss my progress (and she will provide help in any way possible). Finally, I agree to complete this contract on or before Thursday, March 2, at 9:00 AM. On this date, I will turn in my book, my contract, and my completed work.

(x) _____

(x) _____

(x) _____

A. Survival unit contract

Story Activities

1. Draw a map of the area your character is surviving in, and be sure to include places where important events take place.
2. Draw and describe five different tools each character had or made to survive.
3. In a one-page paper explain how the seasons were important to your story. How did they affect the actions of the main character?
4. Create a cookbook of at least five different recipes of foods your character made. Include ingredients and cooking directions the way your character cooked in the book. You can also add some of your own directions. Be creative.
5. Build a scale model of the shelter your character made for himself or herself to live in.
6. Conduct an author study by researching Jean Craighead George or Gary Paulsen. Included should be things that influenced your author, recurrent themes in their books, or any other relevant background information. After you have gathered the information, write a letter to your readers by pretending to be the author.
7. Create a new ending to your story.

Character Activities

1. Create a biographical poem for your main character.
2. Create a character pyramid.
3. In a one-page paper, explain how your character changed and grew throughout the story.

Vocabulary Activities

1. Create a glossary/dictionary of at least fifteen important words for your story.
2. Complete an acrostic puzzle of important vocabulary from your story.

B. Menu list for survival unit

Groups	Cycle Day 1	Cycle Day 2	Cycle Day 3	Cycle Day 4
1. Jaclyn Angie Denis Mike W. Jamie	Discussion day meet w/Miss Grey	Journal day	Journal day	Journal day
2. Brian Alex Kyle B. Mike T. Kyle C.	Journal day	Discussion day meet w/Miss Grey	Journal day	Journal day
3. Bethany Liz Karin Matt Jen S.	Journal day	Journal day	Discussion day meet w/Miss Grey	Journal day
4. Kyle M. Jason Laurianne Jen E. Ashley	Journal day	Journal day	Journal day	Discussion day meet w/Miss Grey

C. Group rotation for survival contract

©2003 by Scott Greenwood from *On Equal Terms*. Portsmouth, NH: Heinemann.

Reader's Workshop Contract

Student Responsibilities

The following will be completed in connection with two self-chosen books of at least 150 pages in length by May 24.

- One double-entry journal response per five chapters (ending with a HOT [Higher Order Thinking]) example.
- One summary sheet at the end of each story.
- One culminating activity from the language arts menu for each story.
- Process log so Mr. B. can monitor progress and pacing.

Title 1: _____

       (x) _____ teacher initials

       (x) _____ teacher initials

Title 2: _____

       (x) _____ teacher initials

       (x) _____ teacher initials

I understand that I will be given plenty of class time to make progress, but that home reading is encouraged and expected. I may renegotiate at teacher discretion.

       (x) _____ . Signature of Student

Reader's workshop contract

Language Arts Menu

- Crossword

- Book review

- Collage

- Journal writing (beyond nonnegotiable)

- Original poetry

- Author research (related to topic)

- Other research (related to topic)

- Original trivia questions and answers

- Create a game

- Vocabulary idea _____

- Character idea   _____

- Author report card

- Character diary

- Setting map

- Your idea _____

Grade six menu example

Partner Contract
Science Fiction/Fantasy

Contract Parameters

I, _____, being an expert at contract negotiations,

propose that I will read _____ by

_____ on page _____ of the *Treasures* anthology.

After reading, I will complete _____ (the written activity at
the end of the selection). I will use all aspects of the writing process to complete my writing activity, and it will be done to the best of my ability.

_____ (partner) and I will read _____ by

_____. We will maintain the same pace and help each other
with reading the comprehension.

> **Partner Negotiable**
> Present fifteen new and interesting words that were presented in your
> book. We plan to _____ to show our
> understanding of our fifteen new words.

> **Partner Nonnegotiable**
> Create and share a Movie Cut-out/Oversized Poster display.

All work is to be turned in to Mr. B. exactly fifteen school days from the start
date.

Start _____/_____   Due _____/_____

Example of grade six partner contract

©2003 by Scott Greenwood from *On Equal Terms*. Portsmouth, NH: Heinemann.

Sounder Contract

We, _____, being of sound minds and
                         (team name)
cooperating spirits, agree to do _____ as a Team.
                                          (activity 1)

We will use this _____ to demonstrate our
                          (project choice)
understanding of *Sounder* and to share its merits with our classmates. We
promise to do all of this to be the best of our abilities.

We have reviewed the Group Project Rubric. We understand that the four
criteria will be developed cooperatively.

As seasoned contracting veterans, we know what we gotta do to get it done!

(x) _____ (team name)

(x) _____ (individual name)

A. *Sounder* contract—group example

Group Reading Project Menu

1. Museum

2. Commercial

3. Act out a scene from the book

4. Write and perform a song inspired by the story

5. Create a photo journal (a photo album with explanations)

6. Pantomime a scene from the story as a group

7. Perform a puppet show

8. Create your own idea (must be discussed with and approved by Mr. B)

B. Group reading project menu

Learning Contract

I, _____, being of sound mind and body, do hereby agree to complete the following tasks to the best of my ability, by the assigned due date _____. I further agree to continue to contribute to a classroom atmosphere that is conducive to learning.

Nonnegotiable

- Daily SSR (thirty minutes minimum) self-selected title
- "Little Humpbacked Horse" Pack and Discussion _____
- "Ooka the Honest Thief" Pack and Discussion _____
- How-to lesson: "Disasters!" Sample Unit _____
- "Emergency on Avianca Flight 52" Pack
- "Custer's Last Stand" Pack
- 500 words: Autobiography and/or Writing Experiments Pack (proofed and recopied)
- How-to lesson: Create Your Own Crossword Puzzle _____
- Mystery Sentence Edits _____ (with self-check)
- Analogies Pack (with self-check)
- Lesson(s) _____ Spelling: any three workbook activities per lesson (with self-check)
- _____
- Study sessions for completion of previous contract (if applicable)
- Daily recording of work completed in process log
- Submission of all contracted work, along with self-evaluation form, process log, and original contract, on or before due date, in folder provided

Negotiable

- _____
- _____

Exhibition of Learning

To demonstrate what I have learned I will do the following:
- _____
- _____

Grade six, one week, two-hour blocks daily

EXTRA CREDIT

_____

_____

_____

REWARDS

In addition to the points I will earn for completing this contract I wish to receive the following reward(s):

ASSURANCES

- I will stay on task in class, working alone or with my partner(s).
- I understand that work not completed during class time must be completed at home.
- I understand that a heavy penalty will be assessed for lateness.
- I understand that I am free, within necessary restraints, to plan my time as I see fit.
- I will have all formal writing assignments proofread by one student and one parent.
- Contract rules have been explained, and I understand so far.
- I am aware that the contract is worth _____ points.

     (x) _____ _____ (student)

- I will give necessary help and support.
- I will review/correct student work carefully and return it quickly.

     (x) _____ (teacher)

- I will give necessary help and support.

     (x) _____ (parent)

Second page of grade six contract

SELF-EVALUATION

In the space below, please comment on your own performance in each of the following areas:

Overall work quality

Use of time in school

Use of time at home

Ability to work constructively with peers

Efficient use of teacher time

Enjoyment of contract-learning process

Third page of grade six project

CHOOSING TIME CONTRACT

I _____ will
Do these things by the end of this week.
Date due: _____

Read a new book (silently)	Write a letter	Oral Reading – Tape Recorder
Date _____	Date _____	Date _____

Word Sorting	Making Words	Free Choice
Date _____	Date _____	Date _____

Skill builder	Journaling	Computer: CCC
Date _____	Date _____	Date _____

Choosing time contract for younger children

I _____ Jamaal W. _____ would like to improve...

___ my stories by using ___

___ sentences and full stops ___

_____

Date: ___ 2/4 ___

Signature: ___ Jamaal ___

Teacher's Signature: ___ Miss Bilbow ___

— — — — — — — — — — — — —

well done

I achieved this on

date: _____

Signed by: _____

Skill contract

Name _____

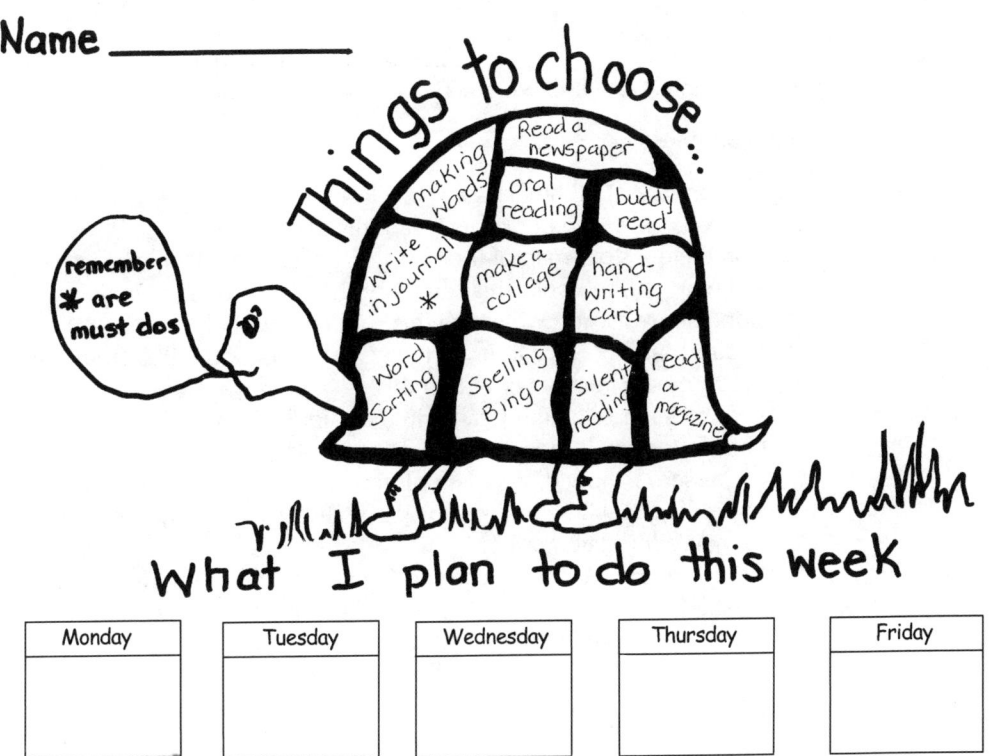

Things to choose...

- Read a newspaper
- making words
- oral reading
- buddy read
- Write in journal *
- make a collage
- hand-writing card
- Word Sorting
- Spelling Bingo
- Silent reading
- read a magazine

remember * are must dos

What I plan to do this week

Monday	Tuesday	Wednesday	Thursday	Friday

Weekly plan

Contract

I, _____, being of sound mind and body, do hereby agree to complete the following activities by the due dates:

A. Nonnegotiables

_____1. Stay on task at all times!

_____2. Choose one of the books you read this marking period. Complete a story map of the book. Use this map to write a summary of the book. This summary should include the major story elements. You will share this summary with the class on Friday, March 27. Try to bring the actual book. You will turn in the summary, neatly written on this date.

_____3. Write a letter to a Fifth Grader in the Middle School. This is a chance for you to have questions answered and concerns addressed. Follow correct letter format. Begin by introducing yourself, end with a thank-you. The final copy has to be turned in by Wednesday, April 1.

_____4. Complete the Nutrition Learning Center activities. Use the check-list to keep track of activities. Keep all completed activities in your contract folder—due April 3.

_____5. Write a letter as Clifford. Original ideas will earn you a better grade—due April 3.

B. Negotiables

1. _____
2. _____

(x) _____
I will do my best work

(x) _____
I will give services as needed

Fourth grade contract

Beta Team LA Learning Contract

I, _____, being of sound mind and body, do hereby agree to complete the following tasks by the end of class. I understand that more flexible contracts with more student choices will follow this year if I do a good job on this one.

1. 20 minutes Compass Work Station:
   Work on the assignments under C-PAS Reading 5.
   If you finish the assignments, being Test B. Remember, when you want to stop, answer the question and click on the Stop Sign. Do not click on the arrow.
2. Michelle Kwan Trading Card:
   The supplies are on the table near the computer printer.
   Finish the worksheet in your Practice Book p. 65.
   Then, do a rough draft of your card on loose leaf. Write out all the information you wish to include.
   When you are finished proofreading for CONVENTIONS, create your card. (One piece of poster board per customer, please. Be careful!)
3. When you finish your trading card, work on p. 64 in your Spelling Book.
4. Finished? Do a vocabulary Builder Crossword Puzzle. Use a dictionary!
5. Self-selected reading . . . your choice!

I understand that this contract is worth 100 points toward my first-quarter grade. This contract has been explained to me. I will self-correct to the best of my ability and 6-inch talk when appropriate.

(x) _____
              (student)

I will continually offer guidance and help and prompt feedback so that students will achieve their best results.

(x) _____
              (teacher)

Fifth grade contract 1

Alpha Team Learning Contract

I, _____, being of sound mind and body promise to do my best to meet the objectives of this contract. I understand that I have 4 days to complete this contract. It is due on February 28, and is worth 100 points. Each completed activity is worth 10 points.

Nonnegotiable: (Things you must do.) Each one is worth 10 points.

Assignment	My Check	Teacher's Check
Finish reading Frindle–the entire book (aim for 2 chapters/day)		
Frindle book project		
Frindle quiz, Chaps. 5–12		
Complete 6 free choice response log questions		
Complete Frindle vocabulary activity		
Compass Learning Log on and complete assigned activities		
Verbs–Complete packet Skip pp. 12, 13, 14, 15, 16, 23, 24		
Mini verb lesson with teacher		
Persuasive writing–pp. 11, 12, 13 in packet		

Fifth grade contract 2

Negotiable: (You must choose 1.) Each is worth 10 points.
*Additional negotiable activities may be completed for *extra credit*.

- Self-selected reading book
- Self-selected reading response journal
- Teacher journal
- Story pyramid
- Literature letter
- Analogies packet

Please write your choices in the "negotiable activities" box.

Negotiable Activities	My Check	Teacher's Check

Signatures:

(x) _____
Student

(x) _____
Parent

(x) _____
Teacher

Grade: Total Possible Points: 100

Points Earned: _____

Grade for contract: _____

Fifth grade contract 2 (continued)